MAXIMIZING YOUR POTENTIAL

The Keys to Dying Empty

MAXIMIZING YOUR POTENTIAL

The Keys to Dying Empty

DR. MYLES MUNROE

Destiny Image® Publishers, Inc.
P.O. Box 310
Shippensburg, PA 17257-0310

"Speaking to the Purposes of God for this
Generation and for the Generations to Come"

Bahamas Faith Ministry
P.O. Box N9583
Nassau, Bahamas

ISBN 1-56043-105-9

For Worldwide Distribution
Printed in the U.S.A.

This book and all other Destiny Image, Revival Press, MercyPlace,
Fresh Bread, Destiny Image Fiction, and Treasure House books
are available at Christian bookstores and distributors worldwide.

For a U.S. bookstore nearest you, call **1-800-722-6774**
For more information on foreign distributors, call **717-532-3040**
Or reach us on the Internet:
www.destinyimage.com

DEDICATION

To the youth of the present generation and their children.

To the readers of my first two volumes on potential, with the hope that you will go on to complete the process you began—to discover, release, and maximize your true ability.

To the human spirit, destined to greatness in its desire to expose the glory of the richness of the treasure of God's grace.

To the millions of untapped Third World peoples throughout the world, for whom my passion is to see them realize their full potential.

To the Source and Sustainer of all potential, the Omnipotent One, and my personal Savior, the Lord Jesus Christ.

Acknowledgments

All that we know is a sum total of what we have learned from all who have taught us, both directly and indirectly. I am forever indebted to the countless outstanding men and women who, by their commitment and dedication to becoming the best they could be, have inspired me to do the same.

I am ever mindful of the unparalleled love, prayer, support, and patience of my precious wife, Ruth, and our children, Charisa and Chairo (Myles Jr.), and am deeply thankful for their understanding, inspiration, and faithfulness in reminding me that they are my number one support team.

To Kathy Miller, my gifted and diligent editor and advisor, who co-labored with me in the delivery of this book. Thanks for your patience, tolerance, and persistence in seeing that I maximize the potential of this book.

To my partners, who with me are committed to reaching the Third World nations with the uncompromised Word and principles of the Kingdom of God: Turnel Nelson, Bertril Baird, Peter Morgan, John

Smith, Fuchsia Pickett, Ezekiel Guti, Jerry Horner, Victor Martinez, and Kingsley Fletcher.

To my hardworking team of partners in destiny: Richard and Shenna Pinder, Dave Burrows, Henry Francis, Debbie Bartlett, Jay Mullings, Wesley Smith, Allen Munroe, Gloria Seymour, Angie Achara, Charles Nottage, Pat Rolle, and Sheila Francis, my beloved sister—all of whom demand the maximum of my potential.

Contents

Foreword

All…that you see I will give to you… (Genesis 13:15).

As we find ourselves in the midst of personal, social, and global change, people experience more fear, anxiety, and hopelessness than ever before. Astronomical job layoffs, family breakups, teen violence, crime, absence of spiritual values, lack of job security, and soaring suicide statistics have created a sense of urgency within people to search for the path to a better life.

In my humble opinion, *Maximizing Your Potential* by Dr. Myles Munroe—recognized internationally as a religious leader, philosopher, and motivational speaker—provides much needed answers.

Not only does he base his principles on the Bible, which is the greatest resource for pursuing one's greatness, but he also lives the message that he writes about.

Born in a Third World country, surrounded by poverty and hopelessness, at the age of 16 Myles Munroe made a decision to be all that God intended him to be. Not only is he a best-selling author and a speaker in great demand, he also travels around the globe teaching from his life experiences and consulting with heads of nations and major corporations. He is a talented singer, songwriter, and composer, and plays several instruments. He is a gifted painter, pastor of the largest growing congregation in the Bahamas, and a devoted husband and father. He is spiritual counselor to celebrities and high profile people from all walks of life, including me and my wife, Gladys Knight-Brown.

Maximizing Your Potential gives you the keys to having the "authority" and dominion given to you by God over every area of your life.

It will give you the methods to discover your life's purpose and develop a closer relationship with God.

Maximizing Your Potential leads you to "seek first the kingdom of God and His righteousness" and, whatever your goals are—whether they're to get your life out of a rut, save your marriage, restart your career, redirect the lives of our youth, and find peace of mind, good health, and financial success—"all these things" and much, much more "shall be added to you" (Mt. 6:33 NKJV).

As we rapidly close this century, *Maximizing Your Potential* will be used for years to come as a torch to lead us out of the tunnels of mediocrity, fear, and despair.

...All that I have is yours (Luke 15:31 NKJV).

> "This has been Mrs. Mamie Brown's baby boy"
> —Les Brown

Preface

The greatest threat to being all you could be is satisfaction with who you are. What you could do is always endangered by what you have done. There are millions of individuals who have buried their latent talents, gifts, and abilities in the cemetery of their last accomplishment. They have settled for less than their best. I believe that the enemy of best is good, and the strength of good is the norm. The power of the norm is the curse of our society. It seems like the world is designed to make "the norm" comfortable and "the average" respectable. What a tragedy!

A quick glance at history reveals that the individuals who impacted their generations and affected the world most dramatically were individuals who, because of a circumstance, pressure, or decision, challenged the tide of convention, stretched the boundaries of tradition, and violated the expectations of the norm. *Few great things have ever been done within the confines of the accepted norm.*

In essence, history is always made by individuals who dare to challenge and exceed the accepted norm. Why follow a path when you can make a trail? It is incumbent upon each of us to ask ourselves the following questions: Have we become all we are capable of? Have we extended ourselves to the maximum? Have we done the best we can do? Have we used our gifts, talents, and abilities to their limit?

Please note that the maximization of the abilities, talents, gifts, and untapped potential that lay dormant in the lives of individuals who have impacted their generations was occasioned by the pressure created by circumstances and situations beyond their control. Unfortunately, the majority of the people on planet Earth will never go beyond "the norm" unless the "abnormal" develops. It's as though ability needs responsibility to reveal and expose itself.

I believe it is our Creator's will and desire that we decide to commit and dedicate ourselves to, and determine within ourselves, to achieve the full maximization of our potential. Once again the questions are echoed: Have we fully utilized our abilities, talents, and gifts? Have we settled for the norm? Have we done our best? Have we allowed others to place limitations on our potential, or have we created self-imposed limitations?

It is essential that you come to grips with these questions because they are related to your personal fulfillment and your contribution to the human family, and to the pleasure of your Creator. You have been endowed by your Creator with immeasurable treasures of ability specifically designed and tailored to accomplish everything your God-given purpose demands. You are equipped with all you need in order to do all you were created to do. However, the releasing of your potential is not up to God, but you. You determine the degree to which your destiny is accomplished. You determine the measure of your own success, success that is established by the Creator's assignment for your life.

Let me illustrate this with a personal experience. A few years ago I was privileged to purchase a name-brand video player/recorder for my family. As I arrived home with my purchase, I eagerly anticipated the exciting process of installing this wonder of technology. My children joined me as I sat on the floor of our living room to open this new treasure for our home. With unrestricted haste, I ripped open the carton and dislodged the machine from its Styrofoam packing, ignoring the manual booklet that fell to the floor beside me. Then, using the basic knowledge I had obtained from others whom I had observed installing similar machines, I proceeded to show my skill and wisdom. After connecting a few wires and turning a few switches, I was ready to test my expertise. I took a video-cassette, placed it in the machine, turned on the television, and bingo—play. As the picture appeared on the screen, I felt a sense of pride and personal accomplishment. Turning to my son and daughter, I said, "There it is; we're in business."

We sat and watched for a while; then something occurred that changed my life forever. The inquisitive nature of my son began to work. He drew closer to the video machine, pointed to the row of 12 buttons, and asked, "What are they for, Dad?" In my attempt to show my fatherly wisdom and adult advantage in knowledge, I leaned forward and examined the buttons. I quickly realized that I was unable to explain any of the functions indicated by the buttons except those of pause, rewind, stop, and play, and I found myself exposing my ignorance to my young children.

I learned a lesson that day that would become a major pillar in my life. Since I had ignored the manufacturer's manual and refused to read and follow the instructions contained therein, I was unable to utilize, maximize, and fully appreciate the full potential of the product. I was settling for less than full capacity. I was a victim of living according to the standards and observations of others. In essence, *the performance of the product was restricted by the limitation my ignorance had placed on its functions.* This limitation of performance can also be extended to those who read the manufacturer's manual but refuse to use the functions inherent in the construction of the product. Therefore, they never experience the full potential of the machine. They only desire to experience the minimum.

In reality, this experience perfectly describes the lives of most of the nearly six billion people on planet Earth. Many live on only four functions: play, stop, pause, and rewind. Day after day they go to jobs they hate, stop to rest in homes they despise, pause long enough to vent their frustration, and then play the games people play pretending to be happy.

What a tragedy! They never experience the joy of the other functions of their lives, such as developing and refining their skills, fulfilling their God-given destiny, capturing their purpose for life, making long-range plans, expanding their knowledge base, increasing their exposure through travel, and exploring the limits of their gifts, talents, and abilities. They have chosen to accept the fate of the millions who have resigned themselves to a normal life, with normal activities, in the company of normal people, striving for normal goals, at a normal pace, with normal motivation, with a normal education, taught by normal teachers, who give normal grades, and live in normal homes, with normal families, leaving a normal heritage, for their normal children, who bury them in a normal grave. What a normal tragedy.

I am convinced that our Creator never intended for us to be normal—that is, to get lost in the crowd of "the norm." This is evidenced by the fact that among the 5.8 billion people on this planet, no two individuals are alike; their fingerprints, genetic code, and chromosome combinations are all distinct and unique. In reality, God created all people to be originals, but we continue to become copies of others. Too often we are so preoccupied with trying to fit in, that we never stand out.

You were designed to be distinctive, special, irreplaceable, and unique, so refuse to be "normal"! Go beyond average! Do not strive to be accepted, rather strive to be yourself. Shun the minimum; pursue the maximum. Utilize all your functions—maximize yourself! Use yourself up for the glory of your Creator. I admonish you: *Die empty. Die fulfilled by dying unfilled.*

This book is written for the "normal" person who wishes to exceed the norm. It is for the "ordinary" individual who has determined to be "extra-ordinary." It is for the individual just like you who knows that somewhere deep inside, there is still so much you have not released: so much yet to do, so much left to expose, so much to maximize.

Live life with all your might; give it all you have. Do it until there is nothing left to do because you have become all you were created to be, done all you were designed to do, and given all you were sent to give. Be satisfied with nothing less than your best.

**Whatever your hands find to do,
do it with all your might unto the Lord.**

INTRODUCTION

One of the greatest tragedies in life is to watch potential die untapped. A greater tragedy is to watch potential live unreleased. How sad to know that the majority of the people on this planet will never discover who they really are, while others will settle for only a portion of their true self. Only a select few will make the quality decision to maximize every fiber of their lives by fully using their gifts, talents, abilities, and capabilities. This we call *maximum living*. Each one of us has the opportunity to pursue maximum living. The question is, Will we choose to exercise that option?

Living to the maximum challenges us all because much of our environment is not conducive to this pursuit. In every society there are traditions, norms, social expectations, customs, and value systems that impact, shape, mold, suppress, control, and in some cases, oppress the natural gifts, talents, capabilities, and potential of its members. This process starts even from the beginning of life. Even a newborn infant receives subtle messages of community expectations from parents, siblings, and other family members that in many cases stifle and limit the child's awesome potential.

Potential screams for release in the soul of every human being who enters this planet. Every individual is a living treasure chest. Each person arrives like a brand-new product from a manufacturer, equipped to perform and fulfill all the demands placed on him by the Creator. This is the reason why the natural instinct to dream is so pervasive in children.

Dreams are visual manifestations of the seeds of destiny planted in the spirit and soul of each human by his Creator. This preoccupation with ideas and imagination in youth is evidence that we are created with the capacity and ability to conceive visions and aspirations that extend beyond our present reality. Perhaps it is this inherent ability to explore the impossible for the possibilities that Jesus Christ, the most maximized man who ever lived, referred to when He stated, "...unless you change and become like little children, you will never enter the kingdom of heaven" (Matthew 18:3).

This simple yet profound command embodies a principle that captures the spirit of maximizing one's self. It implies that the average adult, through the process of growth and development, has lost the free-spirited, open-minded, inquisitive, explorative, daring, believing, and uninhibited nature of a child. It indicates that the ability to dream and explore possibilities diminishes in the course of growth to adulthood. It also communicates the heart and desire of God our Creator that the ability to dream big and dare to attempt the seemingly impossible would be restored in all men and maintained throughout their lifetime.

As stated earlier, most of our social and cultural environment works against our dreams and minimizes the magnitude and scope of the vision in our hearts. We are trained mentally and spiritually to fear our dreams and doubt our destiny. We are discouraged into believing that our passion for greatness is abnormal and our aspirations are suspect. The result of this human "counter-development" process is that the majority of the earth's population lives under the spell and debilitating power of the specter called "fear."

Fear is the source of ninety percent of the lack of progress and personal development in the lives of millions of gifted, talented, and resourceful individuals. Many experts in the field of human behavior have stated that the fear of failure and the fear of success are the two most powerful and most prevalent fears experienced by the human family. The great politician, King Solomon, states it this way:

Fear of man will prove to be a snare [trap of restriction], *but whoever trusts in the Lord* [in the assessment of his Creator] *is kept safe* (Proverbs 29:25).

In other words, when we believe the opinions of men and their assessment of our ability, these perceptions and opinions imprison us and eventually become a trap that impedes and limits the maximization of our true potential.

It is reported that the newspaper counselor, Ann Landers, receives an average of 10,000 letters each month. Nearly all these letters are from people who are burdened with problems. When Landers was asked if one type of problem is predominant in these letters, she replied that fear is the one problem above all others. People fear losing their health and their loved ones. Many potentially great men and women are afraid of life itself. They never attempt their dreams because they fear failure. Others fail to strive for their aspirations because they fear success and the responsibility and accountability that comes with any measure of success.

Therefore, the potential that is trapped within many human treasure houses is suffocated, buried, suppressed, and lost to the world. Most people live at minimum performance, willing to do only what is necessary to survive. They live to get by, not to get ahead in life. They maintain the status quo instead of raising the standard in life. They do only what is required and expected.

What a sad and depressing way to live. I challenge you to step away from the crowd of those who maintain, and join the few who are committed to attaining their full potential by endeavoring to maximize their abilities. After all, who else can live your life but you? Who can fully represent you except you? I admonish you to unearth yourself and share your treasure with the world.

A few years ago I was invited to the beautiful nation of Brazil to address a leadership conference. During my stay there, my host took me to visit a little town made famous by a sculptor who had lost both hands to the disease of leprosy. As a young man stricken with this horrible disease, he would sit for many hours and watch his father work in his wood carving shop. One day the young man decided to train himself to carve and sculpt wood with his feet and the parts of his arms he had not lost to the leprosy.

The resilient spirit of this young man released his untapped potential, and his work gave evidence that trapped within this cripple was one of the greatest artists the world has ever known. I stood in amazement and disbelief as I viewed some of his magnificent works of wood, installed in the most beautiful churches in that city. We also visited his rendition of the major Old Testament prophets, 12 life-sized carvings that are displayed as one of Brazil's most admired national treasures.

Tears filled my eyes as I was told the story of this great handless sculptor. I could not but think of the millions of people who have both hands, arms, and feet in perfect working condition, but who fail to leave anything to their generation. This sculptor is evidence and testimony that buried within each of us is potential that can be maximized if we are willing to go beyond our fears, to overcome the norms and opinions of society, to hurdle the fabricated barriers of prejudice, and to defy the naysayers. There is no handicap except that of our minds. There is no limit to our potential except that which is self-imposed.

Jesus Christ, the specimen of humanity who best demonstrated the unlimited nature of the potential in mankind, said, "Everything is possible for him who believes" (Mark 9:23b). What daring spirit this statement ignites. It makes us question our own limitations and disagree with our fears.

It is a known fact that every manufacturer designs his product to fulfill a specific purpose and equips it with the necessary components and ability to function according to that purpose. Therefore, the potential of a product is determined and established by the purpose for which the manufacturer made it. This very same principle is inherent throughout creation. The Master Creator and Designer established His purpose for each item in creation and built into each the ability or potential to perform and fulfill that purpose or assignment. For example, the purpose for seeds is to produce plants; therefore, by design, all seeds possess the ability and potential to produce plants. This ability to reproduce does not, however, guarantee that the seed will produce a plant. This is the tragedy of nature. The destruction of a seed is in essence the termination of a forest.

This principle can be applied to all God's created beings. For example, your life is a result of a purpose in the mind of God that requires your existence. You were created because there is something God wants done that demands your presence on this planet. You were designed and dispatched for destiny. This destiny and purpose is also the key to your ability. You were created with the inherent abilities, talents, gifts, and inclinations to fulfill this purpose. Just as a bird is designed to fly, a fish to swim, and an apple tree to bear fruit, even so you possess the potential to be all you were born to be. Your life has the potential to fulfill your purpose.

You, and every other individual, possess the responsibility for this awesome treasure buried within, because this treasure within you can be fully released only if you are willing to believe and accept God's dream for your life. If you are willing to submit to His will and purpose for your destiny and to cooperate with His specifications, nothing will be impossible for you.

Determine not to be satisfied with anything less than the full accomplishment of your dream. Surrender to the demands that maximize your potential so that none of your assignment is left undone when you leave this planet. The responsibility to use what God has stored within you is yours alone.

Many individuals are aware of their ability and potential, but they have become frustrated and disillusioned by either their past failures or the negative influence of others. They have chosen to limit or withhold the wonderful gift the Creator has invested in them. Therefore, I strongly urge you to rise up from your temporary fears, shake yourself, and step out once again on the road to being and becoming your true self.

Man is like an onion.
His potential is exposed one layer at a time
until all he is, is known by all.

CHAPTER ONE

WHY MAXIMIZE?

**Nothing is more irritating, guilt-producing,
and incriminating than an unfinished book;
live to your last chapter.**

It was four o'clock on a cold, wet, winter morning. The snow had turned to mush, the wind blew with a vengeance, and the entire day seemed destined to be a source of depression. The small town appeared to be drugged as farmers, storekeepers, and street sweepers dragged themselves to their places of business. Suddenly, a young boy about 12 years of age appeared on the time-weathered, cobble-stoned sidewalk, skipping along as he clutched an old cello case. The smile and quick stride revealed his anxiety and anticipation of reaching his intended destination.

The little boy's name was Pablo Casals. His interest in and commitment to music at such an early age inspired even his teacher and proved to be the seed of destiny for one of the world's greatest cellists. Through the years, his work, accomplishments, and achievements have been testimonies of greatness that stand worthy of emulation. Millions have enjoyed his live performances; history will always hold a place for his ineffable work.

Yet, after a lifetime of distinguished achievements, Pablo Casals, at age 85, continued to rise early and spend most of the day practicing his cello. When he was asked during an interview why he continued to practice five hours a day, Casals replied, "Because I think I'm getting better."

Great minds and souls, knowing always that what they have done must never be confused with what they can yet do, never settle for great work. As a matter of fact, the concept of retirement is a great myth that traps the untapped potential buried in millions of talented, gifted, and valuable individuals. This Western concept has caused many great men and women to settle for the average and to succumb to the mediocrity of the socially accepted standards of success. Please note, however, that all individuals throughout history who have left their footprints in the sands of destiny were driven by a passion greater than the desire for personal comfort.

Pablo Casals reminds us of the monumental character of men and women such as Abraham, the biblical patriarch who at 70 years of age, childless and frustrated, married to a barren woman, and being, with his wife, beyond the biological age of conceiving a child, accepted the vision of a baby destined to change the world and believed it would come to pass. Abraham saw the fruit of his faith when he was 100 years old.

Moses, at midlife, changed careers from a sheep-herding fugitive to a deliverer and national leader of over three million people; by age 120 he had guided them safely to the brink of their destiny. David, the great king of Israel, worked in the twilight of his many years of excellent leadership to make plans for the construction of a magnificent temple for worship, a temple that was eventually built by his son Solomon. Paul, the unrivaled apostle of the Church, after many years of tremendous hardship, wrote a brief description of his challenges in a letter to the church at Corinth. He stated:

I have worked much harder, been in prison more frequently, been flogged more severely, and been exposed to death again and again. Five times I received from the Jews the forty lashes minus one. Three times I was beaten with rods, once I was stoned, three times I was shipwrecked, I spent a night and a day in the open sea, I have been constantly on the move. I have been in danger from rivers, in danger from bandits, in danger from my own countrymen, in danger from Gentiles; in danger in the city, in danger in the country, in danger at sea; and in danger from false brothers. I have labored and toiled and have often gone without sleep; I have known hunger and thirst and have often gone without food; I have been cold and naked (2 Corinthians 11:23b-27).

Then this great leader exclaims: "Who is weak, and I do not feel weak?" (2 Corinthians 11:29a)

Retirement was never a concept in the minds of these world changers. As a matter of fact, the apostle Paul, while spending his final days in prison under house arrest by order of the government of Rome, refused to retire or succumb to the environmental restrictions of age, imprisonment, and threats. Instead, he spent the rest of his days writing beautiful, life-changing, historical documents that constitute three-quarters of the New Testament and form the basis of most of the doctrine of the Christian Church today.

**Retirement is never a concept
in the minds of world changers.**

Like Pablo Casals, the apostle Paul believed that no matter what he had done, accomplished, achieved, or experienced in the past, there was always so much more left within to develop, release, and express. They both believed that the enemy of better is best, and the tomb of the extra-ordinary is the ordinary.

∞ LIFE IS BUT A CUP OF DRINK ∞

Paul's perception of life, and the responsibility of each of us to maximize life to its fullest potential, is expressed in his final letter to Timothy. To this favorite young student, he wrote:

For I am already being poured out like a drink offering, and the time has come for my departure. I have fought the good fight, I have finished the race, I have kept the faith (2 Timothy 4:6-7).

Paul likened his life to the ceremonial drink offering administered by the priest in the Old Testament rituals of the temple, in which the priest filled a cup with wine and ceremonially poured it out at intervals in the service until the cup was completely empty. Using this example, Paul gives a very effective illustration of how our lives should be lived.

Your life is like a cup of drink served to the world by our great Creator. The drink is the awesome, untapped, valuable, destiny-filled treasure, gifts, and talents of potential buried within you. Every minute, day, month, and year is an interval of opportunity provided by God for the pouring out of another portion of yourself until you have exposed all His precious treasure that makes you unique. This is called *maximum living*.

True success is not a project but a journey. The spirit of achievement is guided by the notion that success is an installment plan on which we make daily payments until we maximize ourselves. This success begins when we understand and accept that life is a process of growing and developing. Thus, life is meant to be a never-ending education, a journey of discovery and adventure, an exploration into our God-given potential for His glory.

∽ THE MAXIMUM OF MEDIOCRITY ∽

What does it mean to maximize? What is maximum? The word *maximum* may be defined as "supreme, greatest, highest, and ultimate." It is synonymous with such concepts as pinnacle, preeminence, culmination, apex, peak, and summit. It implies the highest degree possible. Just a brief look at these concepts immediately convicts us of the many opportunities we have abused and forfeited because we have failed or have refused to give our all.

This failure to do our best, to go beyond the expectations of others, to express ourselves fully, to live up to our true potential, to extend ourselves to the limit of our abilities, to give it all we have, to satisfy our own convictions, is called *mediocrity*. Simply put, *mediocrity* is living below our known, true potential. It is accepting the norm, pleasing the status quo, and doing what we can get by with. Therefore, to *maximize* is to express, expose, experience, and execute all the hidden, God-given abilities, talents, gifts, and potential through God's vision breathed in our souls to fulfill His purpose for our lives on earth.

> **_Mediocrity_ is living below our known, true potential.**

How tragic that most of the nearly six billion people on this planet will settle for an average life limited only by their unwillingness to extend themselves to the summit of their own selves. Anything less than maximum is mediocrity. In other words, *mediocrity* may be defined as the region of our lives bounded on the north by compromise, on the south by indecision, on the east by past thinking, and on the west by a lack of vision. Mediocrity is the spirit of the average, the anthem of the norm, and the heartbeat of the ordinary. Mediocrity is so common and pervasive that those who are labeled as genius or exceptional have to do only a little extra.

Remember, we were created to be above average, unnormal, and extraordinary. God never intended for success in our lives to be measured by the opinion of others or the standards set by the society in which we live. In fact, the Scriptures instruct us *not* to "conform any longer to the pattern [standards] of this world, but [to] be transformed by the renewing of [our] mind" (Romans 12:2a). To maximize ourselves, we will find it necessary to declare independence from the world of the norm and to resist the gravity of the average in order to enjoy the outer limits of the new frontiers of our abilities. Why do so many of us settle for mediocrity? The answer is found in what I call the curse of comparison.

∽ The Curse of Comparison ∽

A few years ago I was invited to speak at a series of seminars in Germany for a period of three months. I lived with a wonderful family, who hosted my wife and me. During that time I was able to experience the rich heritage and culture of Deutschland. Among the many wonderful memories I still carry is a lesson I learned about the principle of maximization. It occurred during my first personal experience with Germany's world-famous autobahn (expressway).

The autobahn is a network of roads, without speed restrictions, that crisscross Germany and many other neighboring countries. One day as we were traveling from a city in northern Germany to the south, my host asked if I would like to experience driving without a speed limitation. This felt like a dream come true, so after filling up with petrol, I took the driver's seat and entered the autobahn.

At first I was excited, thrilled, and anxious as I felt adrenaline rush through my entire body. The feeling of having the responsibility for power without externally imposed limits also brought other mixed emotions, including temporary confusion. All I had learned from my past concerning speed limits, fear of violation, and restrictions imposed by the law as I knew it began to wrestle with my newly found freedom. In essence, the possibility of using maximum power was challenged by my learned knowledge of limitation. I was trapped by the conditioning of my past and handicapped by the fear of unlimited possibilities.

As the pressure of my foot accelerated the engine, I glanced down at the speedometer and noted that it was registering 80 mph. Being an experienced driver for more than 25 years, I must confess that I had previously driven over 80 mph and had even flirted with 90 mph on occasion. Now, here I was with an open invitation to maximize the ability of the car. As other cars raced passed me with the ease of a low flying jet, I watched as my speed gauge tilted past 80 mph. My host smiled and asked, "What are you afraid of? We're still standing still."

Not wanting to feel intimidated by this opportunity, I further depressed the pedal and felt the thrill of a car traveling at 115 mph. Words cannot describe the awesome power and pride I felt controlling the speed and direction of such ability. I was beginning to feel proud of myself as we raced through the mountains and lush green foliage of the Black Forest. I was on top of the world. Who could catch me now? I had arrived. I was the king of the road, master of the highway.

This feeling of supremacy was further enhanced every time I passed another vehicle. In fact, I heard myself saying every time we passed another car, "Why don't they pull over, park, and let a real driver through?" There I was. I had achieved the ultimate. I had set a record for myself. I had passed everyone else. I was the best.

Suddenly, after approximately 20 minutes of driving, a Mercedes Benz cruised past me at 150 mph, seemingly coming out of nowhere. Instantly, I felt like I was standing still. My host turned to me and said with a chuckle, "So you see, you are not traveling as fast as you can, but only as fast as you will."

As his words lodged in my mind, I quickly began to understand the curse of comparison and the limitations of self-pride. From this experience, I learned three lessons that have become the foundations of my thinking concerning success and effective living.

1. The principle of capacity

The true capacity of a product is determined not by the user but the manufacturer. The automobile was built with the capacity to travel at 180 mph; therefore its full potential was determined by the manufacturer. The true potential of the car was not affected by my opinion of its ability or by my previous experience with driving. Whether or not I used the full capacity of the car's engine did not reduce its potential capacity.

The same principle applies to your life. God created you like He did everything else, with the capacity to fulfill your purpose. Therefore, your true capacity is not limited, reduced, or altered by the opinion of others or your previous experience. You are capable of attaining the total aptitude given to you by your Creator to fulfill His purpose for your life. Therefore, *the key to maximizing your full potential is to discover the purpose or reason for your life and commit to its fulfillment at all cost.*

> **Your true capacity is not limited, reduced,
> or altered by the opinion of others
> or your previous experience.**

The apostle Paul, in a letter to the church at Corinth, spoke of the hidden secret wisdom of our destiny that is invested in each of us by our Creator God.

> *No, we speak of God's secret wisdom, a wisdom that has been hidden and that God destined for our glory before time began. None of the rulers of this age understood it, for if they had, they would not have crucified the Lord of glory. However, as it is written: "No eye has seen, no ear has heard, no mind has conceived what God has prepared for those who love Him"* (1 Corinthians 2:7-9).

The implication in verse 9 is that no human has the right or the ability to fully determine or measure the capacity of the potential you possess.

2. The principle of comparison.

One of the most significant mistakes humans make is comparison—the measuring of oneself against the standards, work, or accomplishments of another. This exercise is fruitless, demeaning, and personally tragic because it places our true potential at the mercy of others, giving them the right to determine and define our success.

When I was driving on the autobahn, I was in a position of great success and achievement if I compared myself to the drivers I overtook. Yet, even though I was leading all the others, I was still not operating at *my car's* full potential. The car's true capacity was 180 mph, and I was traveling at 115 mph. When I compared my car's performance to all the others, I was leading the pack; I could have been considered a success in their eyes because I was traveling faster than all of them. When I compared my car's performance to its true capacity, however, I was not truly successful because I was traveling below the maximum speed built into the car by the manufacturer.

The lesson here is that true success is not measured by how much you have done or accomplished compared to what others have done or accomplished; true success is what you have done compared to what you could have done. In other words, living to the maximum is competing with yourself. It's living up to your own true standards and capabilities. *Success is satisfying your own personal passion and purpose in pursuit of personal excellence.* In fact, you must always remember to perform for an audience of one, the Lord your Creator.

**True success is what you have done
compared to what you could have done.**

Consciously applying this principle to our lives can do much to free us from the immobilizing culture and environment of our society, which strives to control us through comparison. From the early years of childhood, we are compared to our sisters and brothers, the neighbor's children, or some other person. This comparative spirit continues on into our teen and adult years, developing into a sophisticated dehumanizing state of competition. The result is traumatizing because we spend most of our lives trying to compete with others, comparing our achievements with those of our peers, and attempting to live up to their standards of acceptance. Instead of being ourselves, we become preoccupied with being who others dictate we should be.

If we succumb to this temptation, we will be reminded, just like the Mercedes Benz reminded me of my mediocrity, that there will always be some people whom we exceed and others who outpace us. If we compete with ourselves and not with others, then it does not matter who is behind us or ahead of us; our goal is to become and achieve all we are capable of being and doing, and this becomes the measure of our satisfaction.

The apostle Paul, the great leader of the Church, commented on this critical issue:

We do not dare to classify or compare ourselves with some who commend themselves. When they measure themselves by themselves and compare themselves with themselves, they are not wise. We, however, will not boast beyond proper limits, but will confine our boasting to the field God has assigned to us... (2 Corinthians 10:12-13).

To his friends in Galatia Paul further reiterates this principle by declaring,

If anyone thinks he is something when he is nothing, he deceives himself. Each one should test his own actions. Then he can take pride in himself, without comparing himself to somebody else, for each one should carry his own load [responsibility] (Galatians 6:3-5).

These statements strongly admonish us not to compete with others or to compare our talents with their abilities or potential, since we are responsible only for our potential, not theirs. The story of the servants with the talents clearly confirms this personal responsibility (see Matthew 25:14-30). Therefore, our principal goal in life should be to discover God's will and purpose for our lives and to complete our assignment with excellence.

3. The principle of experience.

Experience may be defined as "the observation of facts as a source of knowledge and skill gained by contact with facts and events." By its very nature, experience is a product of the past and is, therefore, limited to and controlled by previous exposure. In spite of the fact that experience may be valuable for making decisions and judgments concerning the future, it is important to know that any significant measurement of growth, development, expansion, or advancement will require experience to submit to the substance of the unknown through faith.

Unfortunately, experience has compelled many promising people to cower in the shadows of fear and failure because they were not willing to venture out into the uncharted frontiers of new possibilities. Experience is given not to determine the limits of our lives, but to create a better life for us. Experience is a tool to be used!

My experience with driving over the years had conditioned me to drive a car monitored by the speed limits established by the society. Therefore, my driving capacity had become subject to the accepted norms of 45-60 mph. The fact that I have driven my cars at 45-60 mph for over 25 years does not cancel the automobile's capacity to travel at 100-180 mph. *In essence, experience does not cancel capacity.*

Therefore, my car's capacity is determined not by my use of that capacity but by the capacity built into the car by the manufacturer.

Experience does not cancel capacity.

This is also true of our lives. At any point in our lives, we are the sum total of all the decisions we have made, the people we have met, the exposure we have had, and the facts we have learned. In essence, every human is a walking history book. Nevertheless, we must keep in mind that our personal history is being made and recorded every day, and our past experience was once our future. Therefore, we must be careful not to allow our past to determine the quality of our future. Instead, we must use our experience to help us make better decisions, always guarding against the possibility that it may limit our decisions. *Remember, your ability is never limited to your experience.*

This world is filled with millions of individuals who are capable of traveling at a maximum capacity of 180 mph, but they have settled for 55 mph. Because they have overtaken some folks or have exceeded the expectations of a few others, they have compared their lives to these persons and have accepted mediocrity as excellence.

Determine not to let your past experience limit your capacity. Be grateful for the lessons of the past, then accelerate with confidence on to the autobahn of life, being careful to obey only those signs that have been established by your Creator, who admonishes you, "All things are possible if you only believe" (see Mark 9:23).

∞ Dissatisfaction With a Fraction ∞

One of life's great tragedies is that the majority of the world's population is composed of individuals who have negotiated an agreement with mediocrity, signed a contract with the average, and pledged allegiance to the ordinary. They have resolved never to be more than society has made them or do more than is expected. What a tragedy of destiny. God expects more!

Inside of every human being is a deep call of destiny to do something worthwhile with our lives. The urge to accomplish great things and engage in significant endeavors is the germ of purpose planted by God in the heart of man. Why then do we settle for so little? Why do we abandon our dreams and deny our purpose? Why do we live below our privilege, buried in the cemetery of wishful thinking and empty regrets?

As we have seen, one reason we fail to progress in fulfilling our purpose is satisfaction with our present measure of success. The belief that we have arrived is the deterrent that keeps us from getting to our destination. A second part of the answer lies in the fact that we have accepted the present state of our lives as the best we can do under the circumstances.

This concept, "under the circumstances," serves to imprison us and to immobilize our God-given ambition because too many of us have surrendered to the status quo and have become prisoners of the war for our minds. We forget that "circumstances" are simply temporary arrangements of life to which we are all exposed. We overlook or disregard the fact that these circumstances are designed to identify, expose, develop, refine, and maximize our true potential. It's not what happens to us that matters, but what we do with what happens. Much of the time we are not responsible for our circumstances, but we are always responsible for our response to those circumstances. *One key to maximizing your potential is to become dissatisfied with the circumstances that restrict, limit, and stifle your potential.*

Many people know that they possess great potential, that they have a significant purpose in life, but they still fail to move beyond good intentions to experience the fullness of their lives. Why? Their comfort is greater than their passion. They are more concerned with fitting in than with standing out.

Remember, *you will never change anything that you are willing to tolerate.* Your Creator wants you to consciously choose to fulfill your purpose and maximize your potential because in so doing you will bring glory to His name. Unfortunately, history gives evidence of only a few rare individuals who, driven by a passion to achieve a cherished vision in their hearts, initiated their own deliverance, rose above the tide of the norm, and impacted their generation and ours.

A second significant key to maximizing potential is the unassuming benefits of "crisis." Crises, as defined by author Dick Leider, are life's "wake-up" calls. These alarms are often the catalysts that impel us to become fully conscious of our mediocre lives.

Crises are life's wake-up calls.

How many stories have you heard about individuals who, after a close call with death or disease, suddenly change their lifestyles and their attitude toward life? Often their priorities, and sometimes their entire value system, change. The biblical record bears witness to the efficacy of a crisis to get people back on track. Beginning with Abraham, and continuing on to Joseph, Moses, David, Jonah, Peter, and most significantly the apostle Paul, God used the interjection of a major crisis to lead these heroes of faith to move beyond mediocrity to life at the maximum.

Remember, *we cannot become what we were born to be by remaining what we are.* Just as the mother eagle removes the comforts of her feathery nest to "disturb" the young eaglets into flying, so our Creator moves us beyond our comfort zones so that we are forced to fly. Without this stirring, most of us would never fly.

An eagle that doesn't fly cannot fulfill its purpose. Likewise, your life will lack purpose and focus until you discover your wings. This discovery will require both wisdom and courage because the thrill of flying always begins with the fear of falling. Yet you are not left alone to find your wings because God, through the prophet Moses, promises to undertake for you.

Like an eagle that stirs up its nest and hovers over its young, that spreads its wings to catch them and carries them on it pinions. The Lord alone [leads you] (Deuteronomy 32:11-12a).

He will give definition to the crises of your life and inspire you to move on into all He has planned for you. Indeed, the greatest gift God can offer you is to push you into a crisis of temporary discomfort that requires you to try your wings. This pushing into crisis is His supreme act of love, akin to that of a mother eagle that pushes her young from the nest to force them to fly.

**Don't be a pigeon if you were born to be an eagle.
Experience God's altitude for your life.**

∞ PRINCIPLES ∞

1. What you have done does not equal the sum of what you can do.

2. Success is a journey of discovery and adventure as you explore your God-given potential.

3. Mediocrity accepts the norm, pleases the crowd, and does what it can get by with. Maximum living pushes the norm, pleases God, and sets the standard of excellence.

4. The capacity of your potential is not determined by what you have done or what others think about what you have done.

5. The performance or opinions of others cannot measure your success.

6. Your past experience cannot measure your future success.

7. Circumstances and crises are God's tools to move you into your purpose and the maximizing of your potential.

CHAPTER TWO

HOW TO BECOME YOUR POTENTIAL

**What you have done is only a mere
fraction of who you are.**

Slowly the young man worked his way through the brush and the
young trees that had grown up through the cracked foundation of
the dilapidated house. Cobwebs filled openings where windows had
once been and hornets' nests clung to the scorched beams of the
floor above. A partially burned-out staircase hovered in the corner
and a broken oil lamp lay dashed on the first step. Years of dirt and
debris littered the floor, with an occasional wildflower providing a
discordant note of charm and warmth.

At the base of the staircase, the young man halted. Dared he try to
climb the stairs to the main floor above? He doubted the rotted
wood would hold him, yet the desire to go higher impelled him cautiously on. For years he had wanted to explore this shell of a house,
but his mother had strictly forbade it, reminding him that the for-
lorn gate to the fence that surrounded the property contained a
faded "No Trespassing" sign and warning him that it was not safe.

How long the house had stood this way, he didn't know, for within his memory it had always been so. Today no one could stop him, however, for only a few hours before he had bought the land on which the house stood.

Moving carefully from one step to another, testing each before putting his full weight upon it, the young man gingerly mounted the stairs. Here and there he skipped a step that threatened to give way beneath him. At the top, he paused to survey the charred remains that surrounded him.

He stood at the end of a long room that appeared to have once been a kitchen. Broken pottery and twisted metal littered the floor. A warped candlestick lay on the edge of what must have been the family table. Here and there scraps of material waved in the breeze that blew through the paneless windows. Nearly one whole wall of the room was missing, gaping into a room beyond. Though he wondered what that room might reveal, a step in that direction quickly changed the explorer's mind, for his foot went through the floor. Light streaming from the room beyond suggested that little remained of that part of the house.

Turning to his left, the young man discovered a long hallway with an opening on either side. Here the floor creaked beneath his step, but it did not give way. The opening to the left revealed a room dominated by a massive stone fireplace. Parts of the chimney had tumbled onto the rusted, sooty grate, and the filth on the hearth warned that many birds had built their nests within the chimney's shelter. The only furniture in the room was the crumbling remains of a small table.

The opening to the right, farther down the hall, revealed a small sitting room with the hulks of rotting furniture leaning against two walls. Strips of blackened wallpaper hung from the ceiling, but the walls contained no gaping holes as had the other two rooms. Backing quickly from the room when a rat scurried across the floor through the carpet of leaves that had blown through the broken windows, the young man turned to retreat. Suddenly a faint streak of light at the end of the hall caught his attention.

Moving cautiously around the broken boards on the floor, the explorer moved toward the hint of light. As he neared the blackened wall, he realized that a closed door lay at the end of the hallway. The doorknob turned, but the rusted hinges prevented him from opening the door. Though he pushed with all his strength, the door would not yield. Disappointed, the young man retraced his steps through the kitchen, down the rickety stairs, and through the cluttered basement. As he started to climb into his car, the thought came to him: *That hint of light must mean an open window or a hole in the wall. Perhaps I could see into the room from the back of the house.*

After much effort, the explorer stood at the back of the house, having worked his way under the low branches of old trees and through the overgrown bushes and waist-high weeds that hampered his progress. A single window adorned the back wall. Although direct access to the window was denied by high bushes, a large tree spread its limbs within inches of the cracked, but nearly whole, panes. Inching his way up the tree and out the limb, the explorer gasped with astonishment as he peered through the dirty glass.

This room appeared to have been largely untouched by the fire that had ravaged the rest of the house. Candlesticks stood on the mantle over the small fireplace, the wax from the candles having run down the stone onto the hearth below. Books lay open on the desk to the right and curtains hung at a high window to the left. Although the walls were yellowed with age and spotted with water, they were not black like those of the rooms he had entered. Who would have thought such a room could exist in the otherwise ruined house?

Excitement coursed through the young man's veins. Why, this room might reveal what the rest of the house must have looked like before the fire. It might also provide the clues he needed to determine who had lived here and why the house had been left to rot instead of being rebuilt. Perhaps other treasures awaited him in the parts of the room he could not see, untapped resources that would help him to solve the mystery that had always surrounded the house in his young mind. Wildly his imagination soared as he looked into the unexpected chamber that lay before him.

In time the young man withdrew from his vantage point in the tree. His mind was filled with wonder, for the room held possibilities beyond his greatest hopes. Perhaps it would afford him the opportunity to fulfill his boyhood dream of restoring the house to its former grandeur. Already he was busy calculating how he would force open the door at the end of the dark hallway. Then he would know more certainly the wealth of his find.

Potential. The unexposed, untapped, hidden, dormant revelations that lay beneath the accumulated dust and grime of many years. *Potential.* Strength and beauty that lay unmarred by the ravages of fire, wind, and water. *Potential.* The possibilities for rebuilding after years of destruction, decay, and neglect.

Our lives are very much like this decaying house. The strength and beauty God gave to men and women when He created them in His image and likeness too often are not evident in us. Our minds are cluttered with impure thoughts and mixed motives, our bodies are weakened by the effects of bad habits and poor decisions, and our hearts are warped by misplaced trust and the absence of love. In many ways, we are empty people working our way through the problems and detours of life with little hope that things will ever change. This discouragement and dissatisfaction with life is the result of our separation from God, a separation that came when Adam and Eve sinned by choosing to put their own thoughts and desires above God's commandments and promises. (See Genesis 3.) Every person shares this tendency to establish his wants and will over God's. Therein lies the source of our discouragement and dissatisfaction.

**Our discouragement and dissatisfaction with life
are the results of our separation from God.**

God's intent for men and women has not changed, nor has He taken from us the strength and beauty He gave us at birth. These gifts are buried within us, covered over by the attitudes and assumptions that prevent us from living the abundant life God planned for us. In effect, *many have placed a "No Trespassing" sign over their power, strength, abilities, talents, and capabilities.* Because we have obeyed that sign, many of the possibilities with which we were born still exist within us—hidden and dormant, unused and untried.

∽ Treasure in Clay Pots ∽

The great writer Paul refers to this hidden wealth within as "treasure in jars of clay" (2 Corinthians 4:7). The jar may not look like much, but the treasure inside it is valuable and priceless. In other words, *what people see when they look at you is not who you truly are. You can become much more than you now are.*

Who would have thought that Saul of Tarsus, a fervent Jew who vigorously opposed the followers of Jesus, would become Paul the apostle, the greatest missionary the Church has ever known? Certainly not the Christians he persecuted—they did not expect anything good from him (see Acts 9:20–21)—nor Saul himself. Not in his wildest imaginings would he have seen himself as a servant of the One he despised. Yet, like the old house, Saul contained a dormant wealth that was not evident under the outer trappings of his misguided religious fervor.

That same wealth is present in you. You are capable of more than others expect of you—even beyond your own most extravagant dreams. Unexposed, dormant potential rests beneath the surface of your daily existence, waiting to be discovered and released. Although access to this great treasure has been clogged by sin, the strength and beauty of your potential can be reclaimed. The destruction, decay, and neglect of years need not continue to hold captive the reality of who God created you to be.

> **You are capable of more than others expect of you—even beyond your own most extravagant dreams.**

This untold wealth within you is uniquely yours because God creates no two people for the same purpose. Your personality, abilities, and resources are God's gifts, bestowed on you before He gave you the breath of life, and they contain the possibility for bringing meaning and fulfillment into your life. They are available, however, only to those who put forth the effort to recover them and to use them according to their God-given specifications. *Learning to tap the hidden wealth of your potential is the greatest task and the most pressing need of your life* because if you do not discover how to expose and use this treasure, you will die with it. This wealth, which is the all-surpassing power of God within you, is never given to be buried. God wants you to release all He gave you for the benefit of others and the blessing of your own life. Let us use the stories of the ruined house and the life of the apostle Paul to establish some keys you can use to tap into your potential.

Keys to Releasing Your Potential

The explorer in the story of the old house was undoubtedly excited as he backed away from his perch outside the unexpected room at the back of the house. He had received a glimpse of the house's former grandeur, a prelude to understanding the original owner's dreams and plans when he built the house. That glimpse suggested the possibility of establishing the necessary link to the house's past—before fire, wind, and water had caused major destruction—that would enable him to rebuild the house according to its original design.

Know Your Source

No one knows a product like the manufacturer. If you are going to move from who you now are to whom God created you to be, you too must seek to understand the nature of God's original design for you, before sin ravaged your life. That understanding is not available to you unless you become reconnected with God, your Creator. Apart from Him, you cannot and will not release your full potential because He gave you this potential and He designed you to fulfill it. *You must know God, your Source, if you want to experience a satisfying, abundant life.*

Saul of Tarsus met his Source on the road to Damascus when Jesus Christ spoke to him from a bright light that left him blind. For three days he remained blind and did not eat or drink. He simply waited before God, wondering what would happen next. Then God sent a man named Ananias to place his hands on Saul to restore his sight and to bring the Holy Spirit into his life. Immediately, something like scales fell from Saul's eyes and he could see again. It was during this period that the purpose for Paul's life was revealed to him by his Creator/Source. After that, Saul spent several days with the disciples in Damascus, preaching that Jesus is the Son of God and proving that Jesus is the Messiah.

What a change! Few of us will experience a change as dramatic as that which occurred in the man Saul who became Paul, but a change just as radical—from being self-centered to God-centered—must occur in all who would discover and use their full potential. This is true because *the foundation key for releasing potential is always a relationship with the source or maker of a product.* You *must* have a life-changing encounter with the One who made you if you want to become who you were created to be.

Like the young man who could not restore the house to its former grandeur without understanding the builder's original design and intent, you cannot expose the gifts, talents, and natural abilities that God put into you if you do not become reconnected with Him. All you do and are apart from God will always fall short of the true value and capacity of your potential. Therefore, fulfillment and value are impossible without Him. Only by returning to your Source/Manufacturer/Creator can you hope to unlock His power within you. *You must know your Source to become your potential. This is the foundation key.*

Understand Your Function

The mode of operation for maximum performance of any product is determined and established by the manufacturer/creator, and must be obeyed for maximum benefit. Thus, the second key to releasing your potential is knowing how God created you to function and applying that knowledge to your life. No builder can successfully restore a house unless he first knows the specifications determined by the builder and the features provided by the original blueprints. A shower, for example, may fulfill part of the designer's intent for the bathroom, but it cannot match all the functions of a tub. Thus, installing a shower in place of a tub would change not only the room's appearance but also its ability to provide the intended functions that were built into the original design.

Man was designed to live by faith. *God's original design for men and women calls for them to live from the perspective of faith with eternity in their hearts.* The Book of Hebrews defines faith as "being sure of what we hope for and certain of what we do not see" (Hebrews 11:1). This is God's mode of operation. He is not influenced by outward appearances; neither is His power diminished by seemingly impossible obstacles.

God is not influenced by outward appearances; neither is His power diminished by seemingly impossible obstacles.

The apostle Paul learned the importance of looking beyond what is immediately visible and evident. Although he encountered many situations that seemed to stand in the way of his mission to share the good news of Jesus with those outside the Jewish world, he persevered by focusing on His God-given task and by relying on the Holy Spirit to guarantee the completion of God's plans. Thus, Paul testified, "[I] live by faith, not by sight" (2 Corinthians 5:7).

Your ability to unleash your potential is tied to your willingness to consistently live from God's perspective, which saw Paul the apostle in Saul the murderer. He created you to share His viewpoint. If you allow the obstacles that clutter your path and the expectations of others to discourage you and to send you on time and energy-consuming detours, your God-given talents and abilities will be wasted. *Learning to function by looking beyond what you now see to what is yet possible is an important key to releasing your potential. You must resolve to live by faith.*

UNDERSTAND YOUR PURPOSE

To fully release your potential, you must discover your corporate and specific reason for existence and the accompanying assignment. One of the first tasks of a builder who wants to restore an old house is to determine the purpose for each room. Although this purpose may not be immediately evident, the rebuilding cannot accurately and effectively duplicate the original building if the purpose for each room is not established.

In a similar manner, you cannot effectively release your potential if you do not discover God's purpose for giving you life. Your potential and your purpose are perfectly related because God never requires you to do or be something that is not part of His purpose. Likewise, He never requires something of you that He did not provide for when He created you. Your potential enables you to fulfill your purpose, and your purpose reveals the potential hidden within you.

> **Your potential enables you to fulfill your purpose, and your purpose reveals the potential hidden within you.**

From his encounter with Christ on the road to Damascus to the end of his life, the apostle Paul knew that he had been called and saved by God for a specific purpose: "...God, who set me apart from birth and called me by His grace, was pleased to reveal His Son in me so that I might preach Him among the Gentiles..." (Galatians 1:15-16). Similarly, the apostle Peter discovered his purpose when Jesus told him three times, "Take care of My sheep" (John 21:16; see also John 21:15-18). Both remained faithful to God's purpose, dedicating their lives to its accomplishment and conforming their actions to its fulfillment.

You are like these apostles. You too have a purpose set forth by God and the skills, talents, abilities, and characteristics that enable you to fulfill His plan. Your responsibility is to discover *what* God designed you to do and *how* He planned that you would accomplish it. Until you discover God's blueprint, you will not have the motivation to uncover the potential that will empower you to accomplish it, nor will you be happy and fulfilled. *Discovery of purpose is discovery of potential.*

Success without an understanding of purpose is meaningless. Knowing and cooperating with your God-given purpose is the third key to releasing your potential. He alone knows why He created you with the specific combination of personality, abilities, and dreams that make you the unique individual you are. *You share the purpose of humanity to glorify God by fulfilling your individual purpose and by releasing the power, beauty, and possibilities hidden within you.*

Success without an understanding of purpose is meaningless.

KNOW YOUR RESOURCES

Provisions are given for the fulfillment of vision. Every builder, before he starts a project, both estimates what materials he will need to complete the job and determines what resources are available to him. God functions in a similar manner. As He forms and fashions each person for a specific purpose, He also provides the necessary resources to accomplish His plans.

The apostle Paul knew that God had given him certain resources to help him fulfill his purpose and release his potential. Varied in nature and use, these resources included his tent-making skills, his Roman citizenship, his Jewish education and upbringing, and, most importantly, his faith in Jesus Christ and his confidence that God, through the Spirit, had given him a message for the world. (See Romans 15:15-19.)

Paul was careful, however, to view these resources only as tools given by God to accomplish His plans. Therefore, he always treated his resources as being less important than the One who gave them. His education and upbringing as a Jew, for example, had to be refined and redirected before Paul could use, not abuse, them. Thus, he came to see the law, which had been all-important to him as a Pharisee, as God's gift for showing men their sin and their need of a Savior. (See Romans 3:20.) Resources cannot and should not be substituted for the Source.

You too possess God-given resources. The proper use of these resources will release your potential, but their misuse will destroy you. Hence, you cannot fulfill your limitless potential unless you learn what resources you have, how God intended them to function, and why He gave them to you. *The effective use of your resources is the fourth key to releasing your potential.*

MAINTAIN THE RIGHT ENVIRONMENT

All potential demands conditions conducive to the maximum fulfillment of purpose. Consequently, all life forms have ideal conditions in which they grow and flourish. The apostle Paul clearly understood that the conditions in which we live affect the nature of our living. Light that is continually surrounded by darkness is in danger of losing its brilliance. Righteousness that repeatedly associates with wickedness may, in time, be tarnished. Thus, Paul writes:

"I [the Lord] *will live with them and walk among them, and I will be their God, and they will be My people. Therefore come out from them and be separate, says the Lord. Touch no unclean thing, and I will receive you. I will be a Father to you, and you will be My sons and daughters, says the Lord Almighty." Since we have these promises, dear friends, let us purify ourselves from everything that contaminates body and spirit, perfecting holiness out of reverence for God* (2 Corinthians 6:16b–7:1).

Paul's observations are as applicable today as they were when he wrote them. "For what do righteousness and wickedness have in common? Or what fellowship can light have with darkness?" (2 Corinthians 6:14b) You cannot consistently spend time with ungodly people, or be surrounded by unrighteous behavior, and maintain your fellowship with God. That's serious business, since *fellowship with God and obedience to His laws and commandments are essential ingredients of your ideal environment.* Life outside that environment will destroy your potential because a wrong environment always means death.

> **Life outside your ideal environment**
> **will destroy your potential because a**
> **wrong environment always means death.**

All manufacturers establish the ideal conditions required for the maximum performance of their products. In the same manner, you were created to function under specific conditions established by your Creator. Any violation of the Manufacturer's specific conditions minimizes His intended effect. The laws of God are given not to restrict us but to protect us by maintaining the ideal environment for maximum performance. Obedience protects performance. Disobedience diminishes potential.

As fish cannot live in polluted waters and plants die in parched ground, so you cannot live in conditions that do not acknowledge God as the central, all-important factor of daily life. Creating and sustaining a God-centered environment is as important for your growth and satisfaction as designing houses that fit their climates and settings is for the reputation and the success of an architect. Maintaining your ideal environment is the fifth key to releasing your potential.

WORK: THE MASTER KEY

Dreams without work accomplish nothing. The young man peering into the unexpected room could dream forever about restoring the house, but his dream would become reality only if he channeled his excitement and vision into drawing blueprints and doing the work of rebuilding. In a similar manner, the apostle Paul could not have reached the non-Jewish world with the gospel of Jesus Christ if he had only rejoiced in his new relationship with God, learned to live by faith, surveyed his resources, and sought a healthy environment in which to live. Paul had to work to release his potential and to achieve his purpose.

Dreams without work accomplish nothing.

The New Testament is filled with stories of Paul's efforts to share God's gift of salvation with those who had not heard the gospel. (See particularly Acts 13–20.) When one door closed, he looked for another. When his traveling companions interfered with his plans, he parted company with them and looked for others who could share his vision. Not even riots, beatings, and imprisonments prevented him from continually seeking ways to share the good news of Jesus. Again and again, Paul worked hard—fighting discouragement, misunderstandings, and distrust—to fulfill his commission from God.

You also need to work. *The love of work is the secret to personal progress, productivity, and fulfillment because work encourages the release of potential, and potential is the abundance of talents, abilities, and capabilities given to every person.* When you refuse to work, you deny yourself the opportunity to fulfill your potential and your purpose, and you forfeit the productivity that could have blessed yourself and others. Therefore, you steal from the world. The greatest safeguard against this theft is both to understand the purpose and the nature of work, and to live from that knowledge.

The Purpose of Work

Most of us are not interested in discovering what we can accomplish when we go to our jobs. We go to work only because we want a paycheck. This view of work is contrary to God's purpose for giving work. He is more concerned with our use or abuse of the skills and talents He gave us than He is with our financial wealth or poverty. He wants us to be good workers, not good job keepers. This change in attitude requires that we begin to see work as a blessing, not a punishment.

Work as God planned it was given to man before he sinned. *It is His tool to make us productive and fruitful.* Because God's assignments and activities always involve work, He designed men and women to share in His creativity by giving them the opportunity to work. Even as God worked through His spoken word to make the unobservable visible, so too we must work to reveal the invisible possibilities that exist in us. Although the *conditions* of work changed after sin—becoming painful and requiring great effort—the *purpose* of work did not. *Work is not a result of sin.*

In essence, work is God's gift to help people discover their potential. Until you start working to discover what you yet can be, you will miss the blessings inherent in work. This is true because work profits the worker by...

- providing for physical needs,
- building self-esteem,
- teaching that the discovery and use of talents, skills, and abilities is far more important than the acquisition of money,
- developing an attitude that sees a challenge as a cause for rejoicing because it holds the possibility for success,

- offering the opportunity to transform dreams into reality,
- multiplying resources, and,
- revealing the potential that is yet to be exposed, tapped, released, and employed,
- Work also blesses others as we give generously of what we have and who we are.

**Work is God's gift to help you
discover your potential.**

The Nature of Work

God's work in creation was to deliver the stuff hidden inside Him. He labored to birth the world. This concept of laboring to deliver is the central factor in God's perception of work.

Work releases potential and empowers success. It uses innate abilities and natural talents to share experience and proficiency. It also energizes the world's productive ability and activates man's creative power. In essence, *work brings forth from a man or a woman the possibilities that will die with that individual unless they are activated, performed, produced, and fulfilled.* In the absence of work, strength and energy waste away, dreams and visions wither and die, God-given skills and talents degenerate, and productivity wanes. In essence, laziness, which is the absence of work, aborts potential and sacrifices possibilities.

**Work releases potential and empowers success.
Laziness, which is the absence of work,
aborts potential and sacrifices possibilities.**

Therefore, God's purpose for giving you work is to bless you by calling forth from you all that He sees in you. He designed you to meet your needs and the needs of others through your ability to work. When you see work from this perspective, and you accept your opportunities to work as the gifts of a loving God who wants to draw from you the wealth of your hidden potential, you will find that work becomes an anticipated pleasure to be embraced as an opportunity to find happiness and fulfillment. *Work is the master key to releasing your potential.*

These six keys are essential for the release of your potential. If you disregard even one of these principles, you will limit your potential because the violation of a law always incurs a penalty, and history has proven that these laws are true. Commit yourself today to practicing these keys so your potential will not die with you. God wants all He put in you for the good of the world to be released and maximized. Only then can you truly become your potential.

God works the vision in; man works the vision out.

∞ PRINCIPLES THAT GOVERN POTENTIAL ∞

1. What God speaks to is the source for what He creates.

God spoke to Himself when He created you, so you came from God.

2. All things have the same components and essence as the sources from which they came.

Because you came from God, who is Spirit, you also are spirit.

3. All things must be maintained by the sources from which they came.

You must be maintained by God, your Source. Apart from Him you will die.

4. The potential of all things is related to the source from which it came.

Your potential is related to God's potential.

5. Everything in life has the ability to fulfill its potential.

God built into you the ability to fulfill your potential.

6. Potential is determined and revealed by the demands placed on it by its creator.

God reveals what He created you to do by placing demands on you. You are capable of doing everything God asks of you.

∞ Keys to Releasing Your Potential ∞

1. You must know your source.

God is your Source.

2. You must understand how you were designed to function.

God designed you to operate by faith.

3. You must know your purpose.

God created you to express His image, to enjoy fellowship with Him, to dominate the earth, to bear fruit, and to reproduce yourself.

4. **You must understand your resources.**

God has given you resources of spirit, body, soul, time, and material things.

5. **You must have the right environment.**

God created you to live with Him in a relationship of fellowship and obedience that is established and maintained by His presence, assurance, guidance, and direction.

6. **You must work out your potential.**

Work is God's blessing to challenge and expose your potential.

CHAPTER THREE

THE ENEMIES OF POTENTIAL

Your ability is your responsibility.

The cyclists arose early the first day of the journey. By noon they were well on their way to completing the first leg of their cross-continent trip. As they fell into bed that night, exhaustion and exhilaration vied for attention. The day had given them an exciting taste of the joy that lay ahead. It had also warned them that much hard work lay between them and their intended destination.

The next morning they awoke to blisters, sore muscles, and a spectacular sunrise. Amid groans, teasing, and words of encouragement, they prepared to break camp and to begin riding. To their chagrin, however, two of the ten bicycles had flat tires. Repairing the flats delayed their starting by an hour or more so that the heat of the day was upon them when they hit the road.

That evening as they set up camp, anxiety and discouragement overshadowed the exhilaration of the night before. First, the bikers had been soaked by a late afternoon downpour. Then, the campfire was difficult to start because wood was scarce and what they found was wet. Finally, one cyclist discovered that a strap on his pack was nearly worn through, and another realized that his canteen was missing from his gear. As they huddled in their sleeping bags on the damp ground, each hoped the next day would be better.

Dawn was just beginning to light the sky when an angry shout broke the silence. An early riser had awakened to find the contents of his pack strewn all over the ground. Something—or someone—had gotten into it during the night. The others quickly checked their packs, only to find that some of their food was missing too. Although no one voiced the thought, more than one cyclist wondered if someone was trying to stop them from finishing their journey. It was a silent, troubled group that mounted their bikes that third morning.

Our lives are not unlike this cross-continent bicycle trip. When we come back to God and begin to glimpse and act on His plans and purposes for our lives, we become excited and we anticipate the joys and the surprises that lay ahead. As we meet obstacles and discover the perseverance and hard work that will be required for us to fulfill our God-given potential, our enthusiasm often wanes and boredom or disillusionment sets in.

Then, like the cyclists, we must simply stay with the journey in spite of the hardships and the discouraging situations and events that plague us. Even as a pregnancy is no guarantee of the birth of a healthy child, so beginning a journey does not ensure that it will be finished. *Vision can be aborted.*

The world is proficient at aborting potential. Not only will it do nothing to help you reveal and use the hidden you, it most likely will discourage you by measuring your efforts against its standards for success—standards it made because the world doesn't know what true success is. Beware of these standards and the disparaging words of those who live by them because, if you let them, they will undermine your journey. Then tragedy strikes as success dies in failure, hope dies in despair, and visions die in the absence of confidence. This abortion of potential breaks the heart of God.

Tragedy strikes when success dies in failure, hope dies in despair, and visions die in the absence of confidence.

You are responsible to release your potential. No one else can or will do it for you. Releasing some potential, however, does not mean that you will release all your potential. Redeeming all your potential requires that you protect your potential, cultivate your potential, share your potential, and discover and obey the laws of limitation regarding your potential. These are the keys to maximizing potential.

You can work hard to achieve a dream, but if you do not protect it, cultivate it, share it, and act within God's standards and directives, you will lose it. This loss occurs because knowing God's requirements and fulfilling them are two very different experiences. One is information, the other action. Many times what should have been doesn't happen because somewhere between the dream and its completion our great aspirations are trampled and destroyed. This is the work of the destroyer.

◈ THE ENEMY OF YOUR POTENTIAL ◈

When God placed man in the garden, He commanded him to work the garden and take care of it. The King James Version of the

Bible says that man was to *till* and *keep* the garden, while Today's English Version assigns to man the responsibility to *cultivate* and *guard* the garden. This requirement of God is given to man before he breaks fellowship with God through disobedience. Man is in his ideal environment, being filled with God's power and anointing, living in perfect holiness and purity, and enjoying God's fellowship and presence. Thus, this commandment implies that something or someone was waiting to take or attack what man had been given to keep. The Scriptures warn us of this thief.

> *I* [Jesus] *am the gate; whoever enters through Me will be saved. He will come in and go out, and find pasture. The thief comes only to steal and kill and destroy; I have come that they may have life, and have it to the full* (John 10:9-10).

Satan is our enemy. He wants to destroy the power of God within us so that God's glory is not revealed in us. He who was thrown out of Heaven to the earth, where he "leads the whole world astray" (Revelation 12:9), is out to remove us from the One who is our life and our salvation. He's out to destroy all we could be because he knows that those who become rerooted in God have the ability to act like God, showing His nature and likeness. Consequently, satan comes as a thief to steal our potential because he cannot boldly challenge God's power within us. Our outward container, which is our body, reveals nothing of the treasure inside us. This all-surpassing treasure is God's power and wisdom.

> *The Lord is exalted, for He dwells on high; He will fill Zion with justice and righteousness. He will be the sure foundation for your times, a rich store of salvation and wisdom and knowledge; the fear of the Lord is the key to this treasure* (Isaiah 33:5-6).

In other words, the key to releasing God's power within you is reverencing Him, which is living with Him in a relationship of obedience and submission. *You are filled with heavenly wisdom, but you have to follow God's program to benefit from it.*

Jesus spoke of this need to live in relationship with God when He said:

Remain in Me, and I will remain in you. No branch can bear fruit by itself; it must remain in the vine. Neither can you bear fruit unless you remain in Me. I am the vine; you are the branches. If a man remains in Me and I in him, he will bear much fruit; apart from Me you can do nothing. If anyone does not remain in Me, he is like a branch that is thrown away and withers; such branches are picked up, thrown into the fire and burned. If you remain in Me and My words remain in you, ask whatever you wish, and it will be given you (John 15:4-7).

No wonder satan tries to steal our potential. He fears God's power within us because it is greater than he is. Therefore, our dreams, plans, and ideas are targets of his evil forces. The minute we have a good idea, the deceiver will send someone to criticize our dream because he cannot permit us to accomplish our vision. As long as we are only dreaming, he is safe and he'll let us alone. When we begin to act on our dream, he'll hit us full force.

Our dreams, plans, and ideas are targets of satan's evil forces.

You are responsible to guard your dream and bring it to reality by safeguarding and protecting it from injury and loss. To do so you must understand how satan seeks to rob you of your destiny.

⨳ ENEMIES OF POTENTIAL ⨳

Satan's methods for stealing dreams are many and varied, according to the vision and the personality of the dreamer. Let us identify some of these enemies of potential so you will recognize them for what they are, the deceiver's activity in your life.

1. Disobedience

The Bible repeatedly states that disobedience withholds God's blessings and rains His curses upon us. This is true because disobedience brings into our lives the natural (God-ordained) consequences of our actions. Teenagers who experiment with sex destroy the beauty of the first intimacy that is to be enjoyed between a husband and a wife, open themselves to AIDS and other diseases, and risk losing the joys of youth due to the birth of a child. They also forfeit their dreams to problems in marriage in later years, to serious illnesses and possible death, and to the responsibilities of raising a child before they have matured into the task.

Jonah learned the consequences of disobedience when he boarded a ship going in the opposite direction from the city to which God was sending him. He nearly lost his life by drowning. In a similar situation, Lot's wife, in spite of God's commandment not to look back, sacrificed her life for one last look at the city she was fleeing from. *Disobedience always wastes potential and retards the attainment of goals. You cannot persist in disobedience and maximize your potential.* To maximize your life you must submit to God's will in everything.

2. Sin

Although the effects of disobedience and sin are similar, sin is a more basic ill because it is total rebellion against the known will of God—or to say it another way, a declaration of independence from your Source. The resulting alienation from God destroys potential because we cannot know God if we do not have His Spirit, and His Spirit is the password to unlocking our potential. Sin, in essence, says, "I know better than you do, God, how to run my life."

King David experienced the desolation and death that result from a rebellious spirit when he violated another man's wife and tried to cover up his action by having the woman's husband killed in battle and taking her for his wife. The son born to David from this affair died, and David endured the agony of separation from the God he loved. What the child could have done in his lifetime was sacrificed, as were David's energy and vitality during the months before he confessed his sin. It is no wonder David prayed:

> *Hide Your face from my sins and blot out all my iniquity. Create in me a pure heart, O God, and renew a steadfast spirit within me. Do not cast me from Your presence or take Your Holy Spirit from me. Restore to me the joy of Your salvation and grant me a willing spirit, to sustain me* (Psalm 51:9-12).

Destroying your relationship with God through sin is always suicide. *You cannot become who God created you to be if you persist in rebelling against Him.* Without God's Spirit living and working in you, you will die with your potential. Sin caps the well of your potential. To maximize your life you must avoid compromise with ungodliness.

3. Fear

Fear is having faith in the impossible. It's dwelling on all that *could go wrong* instead of what *will go right*. Although, for example, accidents do happen and cars must be carefully maintained and driven, fear that prevents us from driving or riding in a car immobilizes our potential because it severely limits where we can go.

Fear is dwelling on all that *could go wrong* instead of what *will go right*.

When as a lad, David met the giant Goliath with a slingshot and three stones, he most likely was afraid. Yet because he mastered his fear by trusting in God instead of thinking about all that could go wrong, he freed the Israelites from the oppression of their enemies and honored the name of God. (See First Samuel chapter 17.) His faith in God moved him beyond timidity to power. Fear is seeing Goliath too big to hit. Faith is seeing Goliath too big to miss. Paul wrote to Timothy about this ability to move beyond fear:

> *...fan into flame the gift of God, which is in you through the laying on of my hands. For God did not give us a spirit of timidity, but a spirit of power, of love and of self-discipline* (2 Timothy 1:6-7).

A spirit of self-discipline submits the information we receive through our bodies and our minds to the knowledge we receive from God's Spirit. It refuses to allow our minds to run wild imagining everything that *could* happen and chooses instead to apply God's promises to the situation and to depend on God's love and power for the outcome. Faith, our God-given mode of operation, combats fear and encourages the maximizing of potential. He who fears to try will never know what he could have done. He who fears God has nothing else to fear. To maximize your life you must neutralize fear with faith.

He who fears to try will never know what he could have done.

4. Discouragement

Most things worth having require patience and perseverance. No pianist plays perfectly the first time she touches the keys, nor does an athlete win a race the first time he runs. Many discouraging moments exist between an initial experience and the perfecting of a skill.

Unfortunately, *much potential is sacrificed on the altar of discouragement.* Perhaps you've experienced this enemy as too many sour notes hindered your ambition to practice or the failure to win a prize took you from the race. Replaying the music until it's right and running every day are the only ways to fulfill your potential. Concert pianists and Olympic athletes aren't born. They move beyond their discouraging moments to perfect their innate skills.

The same attitude is required of you to maximize your potential. *God will not give you a dream unless He knows you have the talents, abilities, and personality to complete it. His commands reveal the potential He gave you before you were born.*

God commanded Joshua to be courageous (see Deuteronomy 31:7; Joshua 1:7-8). Even though Joshua didn't feel courageous, God knew courage was in him and commanded him to show what was there.

Those who are under command—military command, for example—just do what they are told. No matter how they feel about the command, they just obey it.

You must respond the same way to God's commands. Even if you are feeling discouraged about completing the task, you must start it. Do what needs to be done no matter how difficult or impossible God's commands feel. Then discouragement will have no opportunity to destroy your potential. To maximize your life you must neutralize discouragement with hope.

5. Procrastination

How many times have you delayed so long in making a decision that it was made for you, or in completing a project that it was too late for your intended purpose? Most of us do this more often than we'd like to admit.

Procrastination, the delaying of action until a later time, kills potential. The Israelites discovered this when they found many reasons why they couldn't obey God and enter the land He was giving them. When they saw that the land was good, with an abundance of food, and finally decided to take the land as God had commanded them, they discovered that the opportunity to obey God was past. Disregarding God's warning that He would not go with them, they marched into battle and were soundly defeated. God left them alone to fight for themselves.

If you wait for perfect conditions, you will never get anything done (Ecclesiastes 11:4 LB).

Procrastination often grows out of discouragement. When we become discouraged, we stop finding reasons for doing what we know we can do. Then God allows us to go our own way and suffer the consequences. Sooner or later, we will discover that we've lost much because we refused to act when God required it. Very often He will find someone else to do the job. Procrastination is a serious enemy of potential. It eats away at the very core of our time and motivation. To maximize your life you must destroy procrastination by eliminating all excuses and reasons for not taking action. Just do it!

**Procrastination eats away at the very core
of our time and motivation.**

6. Past Failures

Too often we are unwilling to take risks in the present because we have failed in the past. Perhaps the first story you sent to a magazine wasn't published, so you never wrote another story. Perhaps your first garden didn't produce many vegetables, so you never planted another garden. Perhaps your first business proposal didn't win the bank's approval, so you never started your own business, and you're still working for someone else.

Failure is never a reason to stop trying. Indeed, failure provides another opportunity to enjoy success. The apostle Paul discovered the truth of this when he met Jesus and turned from persecuting Christ to preaching the good news of God's salvation in Him.

...I press on to take hold of that for which Christ Jesus took hold of me. Brothers, I do not consider myself yet to have taken hold of it. But one thing I do: Forgetting what is behind and straining toward what is ahead, I press on toward the goal to win the prize for which God has called me heavenward in Christ Jesus. All of us who are mature should take such a view of things.... Only let us live up to what we have already attained (Philippians 3:12-16).

Paul was not unaware of his failures, but he refused to allow them to keep him from doing what he knew he could do. He believed that the God who had called him to serve Him would accomplish within and through him all that He had purposed. He trusted in a power higher than himself.

> *...I consider everything a loss compared to the surpassing greatness of knowing Christ Jesus my Lord, for whose sake I have lost all things. I consider them rubbish, that I may gain Christ and be found in Him, not having a righteousness of my own that comes from the law, but that which is through faith in Christ—the righteousness that comes from God and is by faith* (Philippians 3:8-9).

Paul had messed up, but in Christ he found the reason and the strength to pick himself up and move on. You must do the same or you will never see your full potential. Refuse to be a loser no matter how many times you lose. *It is better to try and fail than never to try at all.* Remember, you cannot make progress by looking in the rearview mirror. To maximize your life you must let the past be past and leave it there.

7. The Opinions of Others

Most of us have had the experience of sharing a great idea with friends only to have them tell us 50 reasons why it won't work. Too often such criticism prompts us to abandon our ideas because we wanted those with whom we shared our dreams to approve of our plans.

Forsaking dreams because others belittle them or say we are crazy for trying them wastes potential. So does changing our plans to suit the ideas and expectations of our family, friends, and business associates. Satan uses those closest to us, whose opinions we value, to get to our potential. He kills our vision by shaking our faith in God and our confidence in ourselves.

**Satan uses those closest to us,
whose opinions we value,
to get to our potential.**

Because the destroyer uses those you trust most to keep you from translating your vision into reality, you must accept that no one is for you except God. No human being can be trusted to defend *your* potential. You alone are responsible. By refusing to allow the disparaging comments of others to discourage you, by removing yourself from their influence when your vision becomes threatened, and by clinging to God's commandments and directions, you can unleash the totality of God's power within you.

Jesus demonstrated the importance of disregarding the opinions of others when He went to Jerusalem one Passover and the crowds believed in Him because of the miracles He performed.

But Jesus would not entrust Himself to them, for He knew all men. He did not need man's testimony about man, for He knew what was in a man (John 2:24-25).

He had a good reason to be cautious about accepting the affirmation of the crowd: He knew the fickle nature of people. He didn't trust their cheers and their pats on the back. Accolades should be appreciated but never required.

The events of the week preceding His death confirm the wisdom of His decision. One day the people in Jerusalem received Him with great joy and hailed Him as the Messiah. Several days later they clamored for His death. Had He relied on their praise and good will, He very well may have lost the opportunity to fulfill His God-given purpose to be the Savior of the world.

You too must beware of allowing the opinions of others to influence your decisions. Do not trust others to work for your good. Too often folks you thought were for you will turn against you and destroy what you have been working to accomplish. Remember, you are required to perform for an audience of one, the Lord Jesus Christ. When He applauds, then you are successful.

Get your encouragement and promotion from God. Tap into the heavenly realm and receive the confirmation of your plans from Him because His opinion is the only one that counts. The opinions of others can destroy your potential if you permit them to touch your dreams and visions. To maximize your life you must declare independence from the opinions of others.

8. Distractions

This is one of the principal enemies of maximizing potential. All of us have had the experience of walking into another room and saying, "Now, why did I come here?" We had a purpose when we decided to go into the other room, but something between our decision to go and the moment we arrived sidetracked us from our original intention. Or we may allow side interests to distract us from our main goal.

Say, for example, that you set the goal of walking three miles every day to improve your health. The first day you walk three miles in a little over an hour. The second day your walk takes an hour, but you walk only half a mile because you keep stopping to pick wildflowers. Picking flowers isn't bad. It's the result of picking flowers—the distraction from your goal—that is bad.

Satan uses distractions to stop our progress toward a goal, or at least to change the speed of that progress. If he cannot convince us that our dream is wrong, he'll throw other things into our path to slow the development of our vision or he'll push us and induce us to move ahead of God's timetable. One of satan's most successful devices is to preoccupy us with "good" things to distract us from the "right" things.

Perhaps God has planted the seed of a dream that He wants you to accomplish 20 years from now. Between then and now He has many other plans for your life. Let that seed incubate, and proceed cautiously. As you stay open to God's leading in that area, He will reveal when the timing is right. Never sacrifice the right thing for a good thing.

Likewise, if God says, "Now is the time," be careful to examine your thoughts and actions closely to see if they help or hinder the completion of your goal. If a plan or activity distracts you from accomplishing your vision according to God's schedule, it is bad for you at that moment. The apostle Paul understood this truth.

"Everything is permissible for me"—but not everything is beneficial. "Everything is permissible for me"—but I will not be mastered by anything (1 Corinthians 6:12).

Everything that doesn't help our progress, hinders it. This is true because obeying God too soon or too late is disobedience. Therefore, we must be careful not to get drawn into good activities that distract us from our overall purpose. God requires our prompt response to Him throughout the journey. Obedience part of the way is really disobedience. We must be true, then, to our whole vision over the long haul because true obedience to God is doing what He says, when He says, the way He says, as long as He says, until He says "stop."

Because distractions take us off course, we cannot maximize our potential if we allow ourselves to be distracted from faithfully obeying Him every step of the way. Even if God, in His love and mercy, permits us to get back on course, we cannot recover the time and effort we wasted being distracted.

God is the only One who knows where you are going and what is the best way to get there. He will not send you by roundabout routes with many delays; neither will He lure you into detours and dead ends. The fulfillment of your potential is His hope and joy. To maximize your life you must stay focused on your purpose and avoid distractions through discipline.

9. Success

Success is another enemy of potential. When we complete a task and quit because we think we've arrived, we never become all we are. If, for example, you graduate from college and teach first grade for the rest of your life when God wanted you to be a high school principal, you forfeit much of your potential because you stopped at a preliminary success. *Leave your success and go create another. That's the only way you will release all your potential.*

Leave your success and go create another.

Remember, satan is afraid of our potential. He knows that God created us to do something great. Therefore, he will allow us a small success and try to convince us that we have arrived. Then, we will not want to move on to greater successes. We must beware that a small success does not keep us from accomplishing our larger goal or purpose.

In a similar manner, we must be careful to judge our successes by God's standards, not the world's. Success in the world's eyes is not really success because the world does not know what true success is. True success is being right with God and completing *His* assignment and purpose for our lives. It's knowing God and obeying Him. Thus, *we cannot succeed without discovering and doing what God asks of us.* Without God, everything we do is nothing.

Therefore, do not be intimidated by your lack of achievement in the world's eyes. The power of God within you is greater than any other power. When you're hooked up to God and you're obeying *His* directives, you will achieve success by His standards. Refuse to allow the world's measurements of success to encourage or discourage you because God's standards are the only criteria that matter. Follow Him as He leads you from success to success. To maximize your life you must never allow temporary achievement to cancel eternal fulfillment.

10. Tradition

Traditions are powerful enemies of potential because they are full of security. We don't have to think when we do something the way we've always done it. Neither do we receive the incentive to grow and be creative because our new ideas may interfere with the conventional way of doing things.

Say, for example, that you are hired to be a receptionist in a manufacturing company. Invoices, orders, replacement parts, personal mail, trade journals—everything comes through your desk before being distributed. Because the company is a large one, you spend much of your day sending out mail or deciding who should receive incoming mail. This prevents you from presenting the company to the public as effectively as you would like and often delays the routing of important contracts and specifications.

Thus, you propose that all outside vendors and salesmen should be notified that their business will receive prompter attention if it is addressed directly to the department to which it pertains. Invoices should be sent to accounts payable, payments to accounts receivable, shipping instructions to the expediting office, parts to the supply room, etc. Your proposal is not implemented, however, because the receptionist has *always* opened all the mail. Indeed, you are criticized for being lazy and inefficient because you cannot handle both the mail and your other duties as the company's gatekeeper. Most likely, it will be a long time before you make another suggestion to improve this company.

The tragedy is that the tradition, which probably served its purpose well when it was started, prevents the accomplishment of the purpose for which it was established. When the manufacturing company was small, it made sense to have the receptionist open all the mail and stamp it received because she also served as the secretary for the various departments. Now that the company has grown and each department has secretaries and clerks within it, the continuation of that tradition is self-defeating. Disorganization, rather than efficiency, is the result.

Remember, no matter how good the present system is, there's always a better way. Don't be imprisoned by the comfort of the known. Be an explorer, not just a passenger. Don't allow yourself to become trapped by tradition or you will do and become nothing. Your present level of success will be your highest level of success, and God, who is not trapped within tradition, will find someone else to do what you could have done. *Use your imagination. Dream big and find new ways to respond to present situations and responsibilities.* Then you will uncover never-ending possibilities that inspire you to reach for continually higher achievements. We are sons of the "Creator," who created us to be creative. Nowhere in Scripture did God repeat an identical act.

Refrain from accepting or believing, "We've never done it that way before." Now is the time to try something different. The release of your full potential demands that you move beyond the present traditions of your home, family, job, and church—in essence, throughout your life. To maximize your life you must be willing to release ineffective traditions for new methods.

11. A Wrong Environment

Nutritious vegetables cannot grow in poor soil and healthy fish cannot thrive in polluted waters. Neither can we maximize our potential in a wrong environment. The apostle Paul speaks to this principle when he says, "Bad company corrupts good character" (1 Corinthians 15:33b). That means, no matter how good our intentions may be, if we get in with bad company, we will eventually think and act as they do. We will not change them, they will change us.

Many dreams die because they are shared with the wrong people. Joseph learned that lesson the hard way. Indeed, he landed in a pit and was sold into slavery because his brothers were jealous of their father's favoritism toward him and they were offended by his dreams that placed him in authority over them. This is really not so surprising because older brothers rarely enjoy being dominated by younger ones. Had Joseph kept his dreams to himself, his brothers' resentment may not have developed into a plan to murder him.

**Many dreams die because they are
shared with the wrong people.**

Remember, others do not see what you see. They cannot completely understand the vision God has given you. Protect your potential by choosing carefully those with whom you share your dreams and aspirations, and by maintaining an environment in which your potential can be fulfilled. To maximize your life you must manage your environment and the quality of the people and resources that influence you. Your greatest responsibility is to yourself, not others.

12. Comparison

Many parents struggle with the temptation to compare their children's strengths and weaknesses with the skills and temperaments of other children. This tendency to compare can be lethal to potential because it may produce either discouragement or false pride. Both prevent us from becoming all we can be. Discouragement keeps us from trying new things because we lack the confidence that we can succeed. False pride short-circuits our potential by giving us the illusion that we have arrived.

If, for example, you compare yourself to an artist who paints beautiful landscapes and bemoan your lack of artistic ability, you may never discover that you have a knack for arranging flowers into pleasing bouquets. The fact that you cannot draw a flower need not prevent you from making attractive flower arrangements. Likewise, you may sacrifice an Olympic record because you are satisfied to run the 100-yard dash faster than your brother.

Whenever you compare your skills and abilities with others—either favorably or unfavorably—you forfeit the opportunity to become your potential because you try to make equal but different people the same. God created you with your specific blend of personality, skills, and abilities to fulfill *your* purpose. To maximize your life you must understand that you are unique, original, and irreplaceable. There is no comparison.

13. Opposition

Satan has a way of snuffing out our great dreams by causing us to compromise. Most often this occurs because we give in to opposition. If he can't stop us, he'll push us to make a deal that is not God's deal. Then we have no hope of attaining our goal because we are trying to accomplish our God-given vision with human values and specifications. Opposition is natural to life and necessary for flight. If everyone agrees with your dream, it's probably a nightmare.

Let's say God gives you a vision to establish an adoption agency to place orphans of war. Because you don't raise the funding as quickly as you had hoped, you become impatient and look for additional sources of revenue. When a local businessman offers his support, you eagerly accept his gifts.

At first this arrangement works very well, but when the businessman demands a position on the agency's board and begins to dictate who can be sponsored for adoption and who can be adoptive parents, you begin to wonder if your decision to accept large sums of money from him was a wise one. Yet, to safeguard the financial support you receive from him, you agree to his conditions. In so doing, you compromise your vision. To fulfill your vision in life you will usually have to swim upstream against the tide of popular opinion. Opposition is proof that you're swimming, not floating.

Compromised vision always kills potential because a vision that is attempted outside God's guidelines cannot reveal His power. Take your dream and be willing to die for it. This is a requirement for maximizing potential. To maximize your life you must accept and understand the nature and value of opposition.

14. Society's Pressure

Finally, pressure from society's standards and expectations is a threat to potential. The word *society* comes from the same Latin root as the word *social*, meaning "a companion," and ends with the suffix *ity*, which means "the state or condition of something." Thus, *society* means "the condition of being companions" and refers to the people we frequently associate with.

The people we associate with, if they make judgments based on age, race, financial status, ancestry, and education, may pressure us to relinquish a dream because they do not believe we can accomplish it: "Your daddy was nothing, so I don't expect that you'll amount to anything either." "You're going to start a business at your age? That's for young people to do." "Only white folks live in fancy houses." "They don't let Germans, Vietnamese, Japanese, Italians, Puerto Ricans...live in that neighborhood!" "You can't manage a restaurant. You never finished high school!" "No woman's ever going to be the president of your country!"

God doesn't think that way. He walked up to Sarah when she was almost 100 years old and told her that she would have a son. Imagine telling your neighbors that you're going to have your first baby at that age. They'd laugh at you and ridicule your dream of being a mother.

Many dreams are killed by laughter and ridicule, but your dream doesn't have to die. Dare to be different. Accomplish something. Trust God's word rather than society's expectations. **Never** *is as old as the first time it changes.* It only lasts as long as the person who refuses to allow society's dictates to squash his or her dream.

Those who say "I can" no matter how many people say "you can't" transform dreams into realities. They have learned the priority of remaining true to their vision and they have developed the inner strength to trust God when society pushes them to abandon their goal. They are those who maximize their potential.

∽ A Treasure Worth Maximizing ∽

When the apostle Paul described our potential as treasure in clay pots (see 2 Corinthians 4:7), he recognized that discovering and exposing that treasure is not always an easy task.

We are hard pressed on every side, but not crushed; perplexed, but not in despair; persecuted, but not abandoned; struck down, but not destroyed (2 Corinthians 4:8-9).

He faced the discouragement, failure, opposition, negative opinions, and age-old traditions that could have enticed him to forfeit his potential and forsake God's purpose for his life.

Yet, because he affirmed that this treasure is the "all-surpassing power…from God and not from us" (2 Corinthians 4:7), Paul persevered to the end. He relied on *God's power* in his life to achieve what *God* had purposed. Like John, he stood firm in his faith that "the one who is in [me] is greater than the one who is in the world" (1 John 4:4b) and his conviction that his Shepherd would take care of him:

My sheep listen to My voice; I know them, and they follow Me. I give them eternal life, and they shall never perish; no one can snatch them out of My hand. My Father, who has given them to Me, is greater than all; no one can snatch them out of My Father's hand (John 10:27-29).

You too must trust God and cooperate with Him to fulfill all the dreams He gives you and to reach all the goals He sets before you. Yes, satan will use the enemies of your potential to destroy God's power within you, but you are not captive to his ways. You can choose to protect yourself from his attack; to cultivate the possibilities you yet can accomplish; to use your talents, skills, and abilities for the good of others; and to live within the laws of limitation that govern who you can become. These keys to maximizing potential, together with the keys to releasing potential, acknowledge both your dependence on God and your responsibility to trust Him and cooperate with Him as He works in and through you.

As we expect a plant or tree to grow from a seed because we know it exists in it, so God calls forth from us the wealth of our potential. He wills that we should bear fruit that shows His potency. Practicing the keys that maximize potential and recognizing the enemies of potential are essential steps in our journey of becoming who we are.

⤜ KEYS TO MAXIMIZING YOUR POTENTIAL ⤛

1. You must guard and protect your potential.

2. You must cultivate and feed your potential.

3. You must understand and obey the laws of limitation that govern your potential.

4. You must share your potential.

⤺ Principles ⤻

1. Vision can be aborted.

2. Satan is your enemy. Your dreams, plans, and ideas are targets of his evil forces.

3. Beware of the enemies of your potential:
- Disobedience
- Sin
- Fear
- Discouragement
- Procrastination
- Past Failures
- The Opinions of Others
- Distractions
- Success
- Tradition
- A Wrong Environment
- Comparison
- Opposition
- Society's Pressure

4. God's power is stronger than all the enemies of your potential.

CHAPTER FOUR

GUARD AND PROTECT YOUR POTENTIAL

**You were created to perform for an audience of one,
the Lord Jesus Christ!**

The boy sighed with satisfaction as the last of the four towers stood firm and tall. Now all he had to do to finish the sand castle was to draw the design on the top of the walls. As he worked, he watched the approaching waves. Before long they would be up to the castle. The surf had been far down on the sand when he started building four hours before, but he had known that the time would come when the waves would approach where he worked. Hence, he had built a large moat with an opening toward the sea to help the water stay in the moat instead of coming up over the entire castle. He hoped the moat would protect his castle for a few minutes before the waves completely destroyed it.

As he finished the last of the walls, the boy also kept an eye on his younger sister. Twice she had come to "help him." The first time she had smashed an entire section of the wall with her shovel before he could stop her. The last time he had been on guard and had seen her coming. Thus, he had protected the castle from major destruction by catching her hand. Now he was especially guarding against her attack because he knew that the time he had been looking forward to the whole time he had built the castle would soon be here. Water would soon fill the moat. Because he planned to play with his boats in the moat of the castle, the boy hoped the moat was wide and deep enough to prevent the first waves from destroying his morning's work.

∽ THE TWO STAGES OF DEFENSE ∽

The boy building the sand castle was wise. He recognized the approaching waves and the misguided help of his sister as enemies of his goal to build a castle and to play with his boats in its moat, and he defended against them.

The defense of something occurs in two stages. The boy's first step was to *guard* his castle by building a wide, deep moat that would keep the first waves from sweeping over it and by keeping a watchful eye on both the waves and his sister so he would see them coming and, thus, have the opportunity to defend against their attack.

Guarding is preventive in nature. It occurs while the *possibility* of an attack is present but before the threat is active and near. Recognizing the existence of an enemy who wants to steal or destroy the treasure, the one who guards watches over the treasure to safeguard it from injury or loss. He does so by taking precautions against an attack and by keeping watch so the enemy cannot slip up on him and catch him unaware. Guarding leads into the second step of defense, which is the action necessary when an enemy steps over the established boundary and threatens the treasure.

> **Guarding** occurs while the possibility
> of an attack is present but before
> the threat is active and near.

This second step of defense is *protecting*. *Protection* is active defense in the midst of an assault. It implements the preestablished plan to preserve the treasure from danger or harm. The boy protected his castle when he caught his sister's hand to keep her from ruining it.

> **Protecting** is active defense
> in the midst of an assault.

∞ WE ARE RESPONSIBLE FOR DEFENDING OUR TREASURE ∞

Protecting and guarding work together. One without the other presents a weakened resistance to the thief who is trying to steal the treasure. The responsibility for this resistance lies with the recipient of the treasure. God didn't tell Heaven or the angels to protect the garden. He told Adam to protect it. In a similar manner, the apostle Paul admonished Timothy, not his mother or his grandmother, to defend the treasure he had received:

Timothy, my son, I give you this instruction in keeping with the prophecies once made about you, so that by following them you may fight the good fight, holding on to faith and a good conscience. Some have rejected these and so have shipwrecked their faith (1 Timothy 1:18-19).

This defense begins with an understanding of the treasure we have received from God and is worked out in our fight to keep what we have received. This treasure is both God's wisdom and power within us (our potential) and the gift of His Spirit.

∞ WHAT ARE WE TO DEFEND? ∞

As we have seen, God deposits a treasure in each person He creates. This treasure is a) God's wisdom and knowledge concerning who He is, who we are, and how we are to live in relationship with Him; b) God's power that worked in creation through the spoken word and even today brings forth beauty from chaos; and c) God's Spirit who lives within our hearts. Thus, God reveals Himself to us and crowns us with His potency—His power, authority, and strength to effectively accomplish what He wills.

But we have this treasure in jars of clay to show that this all-surpassing power is from God and not from us (2 Corinthians 4:7).

This potency of God within us—our potential—is the treasure we must defend. The treasure is the God-invested vision and purpose for our lives, designed both to show His glory and to bring Him glory.

The Treasure of God's Wisdom and Knowledge

The prophet Isaiah recognized God's wisdom as a treasure, as did the psalmists and King Solomon. They also agreed that the fear of the Lord is the key to this treasure:

He will be the sure foundation for your times, a rich store of salvation and wisdom and knowledge; the fear of the Lord is the key to this treasure (Isaiah 33:6).

The fear of the Lord is the beginning of wisdom; all who follow His precepts have good understanding... (Psalm 111:10; see also Proverbs 1:7).

My son, if you accept my words and store up my commands within you, turning your ear to wisdom and applying your heart to understanding, and if you call out for insight and cry aloud for understanding, and if you look for it as for silver and search for it as for hidden treasure, then you will understand the fear of the Lord and find the knowledge of God. For the Lord gives wisdom, and from His mouth come knowledge and understanding (Proverbs 2:1-6).

What does it mean to fear God? The psalmists liken those who fear God with those who "hope...in His unfailing love" (Psalm 33:18), who "understand [His] statutes" (Psalm 119:79), and who "walk in His ways" (Psalm 128:1). They also compare fearing God with trusting Him (see Psalm 40:3; 115:11) and advise those who would learn what it means to fear the Lord to "turn from evil and do good; seek peace and pursue it" (see Psalm 34:11,14). Solomon equates fearing the Lord with shunning evil (see Proverbs 3:7; 8:13) and hating knowledge with *failing* to fear the Lord (see Proverbs 1:29). *Thus, to fear the Lord is to trust and obey Him. In so doing we defend the deposit of His wisdom and knowledge within us.*

The apostle Paul speaks of God's wisdom within us as a "secret wisdom" (1 Corinthians 2:7) because sinful man can neither know nor understand the thoughts and the heart of God toward His children. Only as we come to God through faith in Jesus Christ, "and Him crucified" (1 Corinthians 2:2), and through the presence of the Holy Spirit in our hearts (see 1 Corinthians 2:9-16) are we privileged to understand God's thoughts toward us.

Isaiah acknowledged this difference between God's thoughts and ours:

"For My thoughts are not your thoughts, neither are your ways My ways," declares the Lord. "As the heavens are higher than the earth,

so are My ways higher than your ways and My thoughts than your thoughts. As the rain and the snow come down from heaven, and do not return to it without watering the earth and making it bud and flourish, so that it yields seed for the sower and bread for the eater, so is My word that goes out from My mouth: It will not return to Me empty, but will accomplish what I desire and achieve the purpose for which I sent it" (Isaiah 55:8-11).

This wisdom of God is a treasure to be cherished and defended. His thoughts toward us are good and His knowledge of us is perfect. He sees beyond our vessels of clay to His wisdom within us and calls forth from us what He sees. As we learn to see as God sees and to live from His perspective, we begin to understand this treasure of His wisdom and the importance of safeguarding it from the snares of the evil one. Paul wrote of this to Timothy:

Timothy, guard what has been entrusted to your care. Turn away from godless chatter and the opposing ideas of what is falsely called knowledge, which some have professed and in so doing have wandered from the faith... (1 Timothy 6:20-21).

**God sees beyond our vessels of clay
to His wisdom within us
and calls forth what He sees.**

God's wisdom will never match the ways of the world:

For it is written: "I will destroy the wisdom of the wise; the intelligence of the intelligent I will frustrate." Where is the wise man? Where is the scholar? Where is the philosopher of this age? Has not God made foolish the wisdom of the world? (1 Corinthians 1:19-20)

We must be careful to safeguard His knowledge within us so we can see the perfection and beauty of His plans and purposes for our lives.

Sadly, satan influences many people to close their eyes and walk away from their visions because they don't believe what they see. He knows the potential they contain—what they can become, the many goals they can meet, and the ideas they can accomplish—but they don't. This is why the apostle Paul instructs us to "take captive every thought to make it obedient to Christ" (2 Corinthians 10:5).

When we bring our thoughts to Jesus and make them subject to Him, we combat satan's strategy and unmask his deception. Jesus, who knows both satan's works and the potential God builds into every human being, cleanses our sight and enables us to see rightly through the eyes of faith and hope. This is the beginning of wisdom.

The Treasure of God's Power

God has also deposited His power within us. The apostle Paul spoke of this power as the means by which God works salvation in us—"I am not ashamed of the gospel, because it is the power of God for the salvation of everyone who believes..." (Romans 1:16)—and he carefully portrayed this salvation as "a demonstration of the Spirit's power, so that [our] faith might not rest on men's wisdom, but on God's power" (1 Corinthians 2:4-5).

In a similar manner, Peter and John understood God's power to be the secret behind their power:

> ... *"Men of Israel, why does this surprise you? Why do you stare at us as if by our own power or godliness we had made this man walk? ...*

By faith in the name of Jesus, this man whom you see and know was made strong" (Acts 3:12,16a).

God doesn't want us just to *know* who we are in Him; He wants us to *become* it. This occurs as we take hold of His power and make it our own. We must always be careful "…to show that this all-surpassing power is from God and not from us" (2 Corinthians 4:7). Even when we do not understand how God is working in our lives or what He is trying to accomplish, we can do great things when we cooperate with His power. This is true because potential is vision in a dormant state that can be activated by our faith in God's power. If we are children of God, our greatest goal in life should be to resemble our Father.

> **God doesn't want us just to *know***
> **who we are in Him;**
> **He wants us to *become* it.**

Whenever we see ourselves being something, doing something, or going somewhere, and we believe that God's power in us will bring this glimpse of our potential to pass, we tap into God's power to accomplish His will. This power of God is at work in us to save us and to call us to a holy life in Christ Jesus (see 1 Corinthians 2:1-5 and 2 Timothy 1:8-10).

Satan knows that God "is able to do immeasurably more than all we ask or imagine, according to His power that is at work within us" (Ephesians 3:20) and he is threatened by potential that is transformed by this power. Therefore, we must diligently defend God's power within us so that our vision can be changed into mission and God's potency may be revealed in us. God's power in us is a second treasure to be defended from the schemes of the evil one.

The Treasure of the Holy Spirit

Paul also identifies the Holy Spirit Himself as the deposit or treasure within us that we must guard.

Now it is God who makes both us and you stand firm in Christ. He anointed us, set His seal of ownership on us, and put His Spirit in our hearts as a deposit, guaranteeing what is to come... (2 Corinthians 1:21-22).

Now it is God who has made us...and has given us the Spirit as a deposit, guaranteeing what is to come (2 Corinthians 5:5).

The Holy Spirit both reveals God's wisdom and power in us and guarantees that we will receive all God has planned for those who seek His wisdom and live by His power. His presence in our lives is an important deposit because He is the key to tapping into God's storehouse of wisdom and power. We cannot understand and apply God's wisdom without the Holy Spirit; neither can we live by His power. He is the Counselor to teach us all things (see John 14:26), the Searcher of our hearts to reveal to us the deep things of God (see 1 Corinthians 2:9-11), and the One who testifies that we are God's children (see Romans 8:16). Through Him we know God's thoughts and understand what God has given to us:

We have not received the spirit of the world but the Spirit who is from God, that we may understand what God has freely given us. ... The man without the Spirit does not accept the things that come from the Spirit of God, for they are foolishness to him, and he cannot understand them, because they are spiritually discerned (1 Corinthians 2:12,14).

∽ THE TREASURE OF POTENTIAL ∽

In essence, God's wisdom, power, and Spirit are the treasure we must safeguard. They are a deposit of Himself in us so that we can act and function like Him, sharing in His work. Together they are our potential, the source of our dreams and visions. We must remember, however, that having this deposit of God does not mean that we will keep it.

All the great things God has put inside us—our visions, dreams, plans, and talents—are satan's targets. He is afraid of men and women who have faith in God's wisdom and power, because they take their visions and translate them into action. They not only set goals, they make them happen.

**All the great things God has put inside us—
our visions, dreams, plans and talents—
are satan's targets.**

The deceiver fears the treasure we possess. His destructive tactics and deceptive influences come into our lives to nullify and entrap all God has given to us. He isn't going to let us fulfill our potential without encountering resistance from him. Indeed, his attack is so severe that Paul advised Timothy to seek the help of the Holy Spirit to meet and overcome it:

Guard the good deposit that was entrusted to you—guard it with the help of the Holy Spirit who lives in us (2 Timothy 1:14).

Have no fear! God has given us everything we need to safeguard our hidden wealth from the schemes and deceit of the evil one. We must be careful, however, not to rely on weapons of human strength and wisdom. We cannot whip the enemy by ourselves, "for the foolishness of God is wiser than man's wisdom, and the weakness of God is stronger than man's strength" (1 Corinthians 1:25). Only as we are "strong in the Lord and in His mighty power" (Ephesians 6:10) can we withstand satan's onslaught against us. The Holy Spirit, sent by Jesus when we receive Him as Savior, is our Helper.

❦ GOD'S PLAN OF DEFENSE ❦

For our struggle is not against flesh and blood, but against the rulers, against the authorities, against the powers of this dark world and against the spiritual forces of evil in the heavenly realms. Therefore put on the full armor of God, so that when the day of evil comes, you may be able to stand your ground, and after you have done everything, to stand. Stand firm then, with the belt of truth buckled around your waist, with the breastplate of righteousness in place, and with your feet fitted with the readiness that comes from the gospel of peace. In addition to all this, take up the shield of faith, with which you can extinguish all the flaming arrows of the evil one. Take the helmet of salvation and the sword of the Spirit, which is the word of God. And pray in the Spirit on all occasions with all kinds of prayers and requests. With this in mind, be alert... (Ephesians 6:12-18).

This description of the armor of God details a plan to *guard* and *protect* your life against satan's invasion. You must understand the provisions of this plan and put them into practice if you want to defend your potential.

RECOGNIZE YOUR ENEMIES AS THE SPIRITUAL FORCES OF EVIL.

First, *recognize your enemy as the spiritual forces of evil,* "for our struggle is not against flesh and blood, but against...the powers of this dark world and against the spiritual forces of evil...." What looks to be a conflict in personalities or a difference in values may well be a struggle on a more basic level. Discouragement, opposition, criticism, and the other enemies of potential are the work of evil forces through those who are close to you. Learn to recognize and combat these obstacles for what they are.

Learn to recognize and combat the enemies of potential.

The Scriptures are filled with examples of satan's work. Moses' mother and sister relied on God's power to save him from death when Moses' life was threatened by the Pharaoh of Egypt's decree that all Hebrew boys should be killed at birth. After his mother had hidden him for three months and she could hide him no longer, she put him in a basket and placed it among the reeds in the Nile River. His sister then watched from a distance to see what would happen to him. When Pharaoh's daughter found him and took pity on him, Moses' sister brought her mother to care for him. (See Exodus 2:1-10.) Thus, Moses was saved from Pharaoh's murderous plan.

Joseph was but a youth when his brothers plotted to kill him. After they had sold him into slavery instead of killing him, Joseph endured many hardships that could have prevented his potential from being unveiled and exercised. First, he was falsely accused of seducing his master's wife and was, therefore, thrown into prison; then he was forgotten by those he helped. Still Joseph remained faithful to God and continued to trust Him. He didn't allow the enemies of discouragement, opposition, and the negative opinions of others to destroy the dreams God had given him.

After many years, Joseph was placed in a position of great prominence because he interpreted Pharaoh's dream. Thus, his potential to interpret dreams and to manage wisely were effectively used, and his purpose to preserve his father Jacob's family in the midst of a severe famine was fulfilled. (See Genesis 37–47.)

King Saul tried to kill David many times. After Saul disobeyed God and God chose David to replace Saul as king, "…the Spirit of the Lord…departed from Saul, and an evil spirit…tormented him" (1 Samuel 16:14). As a young man, David came into Saul's house to soothe him with the playing of the harp. Because he found favor with Saul, David became one of Saul's armor-bearers.

Before long, David ran into trouble. As he became a great warrior and grew in popularity, Saul came to be jealous. One day Saul hurled a spear at David. Another time he sent his men to David's house to kill him. Although David escaped, he spent many years as a fugitive, trying to avoid death by Saul's hand. Discouragement, fear, loneliness, distractions, negative opinions, and pressure from others were all part of those years. Yet, David trusted God to fulfill the promise he had received when Samuel had anointed him to be king. In time, David fulfilled his potential and became the greatest king in Israel's history.

Although death is a favorite way for satan to destroy potential, he will most likely try to ensnare you with one of the enemies of potential. Be alert to recognize these enemies for what they are—satan's attacks on your potential.

EXPECT SATAN'S ATTACK.

Paul knew that the attack of satan is inevitable. Thus, he told the Ephesians to put on the full armor of God so they could withstand when the evil day came. He wanted them to expect trouble so they would be prepared to meet it when it came.

No matter what you do, you will always have critics. This is true because some people cannot bear to see others succeed. When you aren't doing anything, you're not a problem for them; but when you start fulfilling your dreams and visions, you'll attract attention. People don't care about you until you start doing something big.

**No matter what you do,
you will always have critics.**

This opposition often occurs because your critics aren't doing anything. Those who are working out their own dreams don't need to be threatened by your accomplishments. They are too busy to be jealous and too confident to worry how your success might affect them. Thus, you must be careful of those who are doing nothing with their potential. They will be your greatest critics.

Learn to expect their opposition and to rise above it. Refuse to get drawn into their petty quarrels or to allow their words and actions to influence your self-esteem or your behavior. *Every dream you share has the potential to cause jealousy*, so be careful with whom you share your dreams. Sometimes you must keep your dream to yourself because no other person can understand it. Indeed, your dreams may sound funny or pretentious to others.

Just stick with what you're supposed to do until you achieve what you're after, and let those who are going nowhere go there without you. Others who are pursuing their purpose and maximizing their potential will understand your behavior, even if they can't see your particular vision. Find them and enjoy their company, for those who are going somewhere are more likely to support you in your journey. This is an essential factor in guarding your potential.

PREPARE TO OVERCOME SATAN'S ATTACK.

One way you can prepare to defend your potential is to make wise choices. Consider carefully with whom you associate and where you spend your time. Examine your reading material and how you fill your day. Be cautious with whom you share your dreams—if you share them at all.

A second priority in preparing to meet satan's attack is to be sure that your vision is from God. Don't conjure up your own ideas. If they contradict God's Word, you know your ideas are not from Him. God will not deny His Word. False dreams and fake prophecies are sure ways to lose your potential. Satan will distract you any way he can. Prepare for his attack by staying in close fellowship with God and by seeking His knowledge and wisdom.

A third method for fortifying yourself against the assault of evil is to seek God's discipline and direction in your life. Be truthful in your dealings. Act with justice and virtue. Live at peace with others in so far as it is within your power, being careful, however, not to compromise your loyalty and obedience to God and His Word. Seek His chastening when you have failed and "rejoice in [your] sufferings, because...suffering produces perseverance; perseverance, character; and character, hope. And hope does not disappoint us..." (Romans 5:3b-5). God will honor your efforts to obey Him and, in so doing, you will guard your potential.

STAND FIRM IN THE MIDST OF ATTACK.

Sooner or later, satan is going to step over the boundaries of your defense and you are going to be under attack. Then it is time to move from *guarding* your potential to *protecting* it. Paul admonished the Ephesians to stand their ground and, after doing everything else, still to stand. Perseverance is the key. You may not win the war in one battle, but you can stand firm in the midst of each assault.

Abraham, Joseph, Moses, David, Paul—all persevered through numerous battles to emerge victorious. At times they faltered and failed, but they always returned to the battle. You too must persevere when the forces of evil threaten to overwhelm you to destroy your potential. The story of Nehemiah offers some hints on how to do this.

∞ HOW TO PROTECT YOURSELF FROM ATTACK ∞

Nehemiah, a common man, had a job as the cupbearer of the Persian king in whose land he was an exile. When he heard of the plight of his former countrymen who had not been carried into exile and the sorry state of the city of Jerusalem, he mourned for them and asked God to help him return to Jerusalem so he could rebuild the city. God heard his prayer and granted him favor in the king's sight so that the king gave Nehemiah both his permission to return to Jerusalem and the resources to begin rebuilding the city.

Not everyone, however, was happy that Nehemiah was taking an interest in the well-being of the city and its inhabitants.

When Sanballat the Horonite and Tobiah the Ammonite official heard about this, they were very much disturbed that someone had come to promote the welfare of the Israelites (Nehemiah 2:10).

Even though Nehemiah was trying to do something beneficial, these fellows were angered by his plans. So they started to make trouble for him.

"What is this you are doing?" they asked. "Are you rebelling against the king?" (Nehemiah 2:19b)

But Nehemiah was not to be deterred. He gathered workers together and began to rebuild the gates and the walls of Jerusalem. This incensed Sanballat further so that he began to ridicule the Jews:

What are those feeble Jews doing? Will they restore their wall? Will they offer sacrifices? Will they finish in a day? Can they bring the stones back to life from those heaps of rubble—burned as they are? (Nehemiah 4:2b)

Tobiah joined in his mocking:

What they are building—if even a fox climbed up on it, he would break down their wall of stones! (Nehemiah 4:3b)

Nehemiah did not reply to their ridicule. Instead, he turned to the Lord in prayer (see Nehemiah 4:4-5) and kept on with the work. This illustrates the first guideline for protecting your potential. *Don't answer your critics.*

There are several levels of anger. At first your critic may be annoyed by you, but if you persist in your work, he becomes incensed. Sanballat, Tobiah, and their associates became incensed by the continued work on the walls of Jerusalem and committed themselves to destroying the potential of Nehemiah and the other workers who were rebuilding the city.

They all [Sanballat and his cohorts] *plotted together to come and fight against Jerusalem and stir up trouble against it. But we*

[Nehemiah and the other workers] *prayed to our God and posted a guard day and night to meet this threat* (Nehemiah 4:8-9).

Nehemiah responded to this new threat the same way he had answered the last one. He prayed to God instead of answering his critics. He also added a second line to his defense. He posted a guard. This is the second guideline for protecting your potential. *Post a guard to lessen the likelihood of attack.*

When our enemies heard that we were aware of their plot and that God had frustrated it, we all returned to the wall, each to his own work (Nehemiah 4:15).

This reveals a third means of protecting your potential from attack. Allow God to fight for you. The workers stood guard, but God frustrated the plans of the attackers. The Israelites relied on Him to fight for them:

Wherever you hear the sound of the trumpet, join us there. Our God will fight for us! (Nehemiah 4:20)

For a while, Nehemiah and his helpers worked in peace. Yet, they did not let down their guard.

From that day on, half of my men did the work, while the other half were equipped with spears, shields, bows and armor. The officers posted themselves behind all the people of Judah who were building the wall. Those who carried materials did their work with one hand and held a weapon in the other, and each of the builders wore his sword at his side as he worked (Nehemiah 4:16-18a).

Thus, they employed a fourth means for protecting their potential from attack. *Don't allow a lull in the battle to convince you that the war is over. Don't confuse quiet with peace.*

Finally, when Nehemiah's enemies received word that the wall had been completely rebuilt, they sent a message to request a meeting:

Come, let us meet together in one of the villages... (Nehemiah 6:2b).

Nehemiah wisely countered this as well, recognizing it for a different kind of attack:

But they were scheming to harm me; so I sent messengers to them with this reply: "I am carrying on a great project and cannot go down. Why should the work stop while I leave it and go down to you?" (Nehemiah 6:2c-3)

This reply reveals a fifth and a sixth means of protecting your potential from attack. First, Nehemiah sent a messenger instead of going himself when his enemies summoned him. *Stay away from the opposition.* Second, he refused to stop his work to talk. *Don't waste time talking.*

Even when Sanballat sent letters four and five times requesting Nehemiah to come to a village to talk, and tried to intimidate Nehemiah by suggesting that he would soon be in trouble with the king in Persia, Nehemiah remained firm in his stance. He again sent a letter instead of going himself, and he accused his opposers of making things up in their heads to create trouble. You too must *remain firm in your decisions and refuse to be intimidated by your oppressors.* These are the seventh and eighth factors in protecting your potential when you are under assault.

Nehemiah used many methods to fight for his vision. You must employ the same methods to preserve your potential from attack.

∞ FIGHT FOR YOUR VISION ∞

There will always be people who are committed to destroying you. They will criticize you, ridicule you, and become angry with you. Let them. You are not responsible for their actions, only your own.

Fight for your vision. Share your dream only when you must, and choose carefully with whom you share it. Do the background work and stay on course when the going gets rough. Expect opposition and be careful not to allow the threats and accusations of your enemies to intimidate you. Stick with your decisions and remain committed to your goal. Don't let quietness fool you so that you are caught unprepared by a later attack. Talk to God about your needs and allow Him to respond to your oppressors. Never answer them yourself.

Finally, keep yourself busy. *Don't allow the battle to interfere with your work.* You may not be popular, but you will be successful because God works with those who put forth the effort to stay with the vision He has given them. Thus, *your opposers will learn that they are not as important as what you are doing,* and you will remain focused on your vision with renewed wisdom and strength to accomplish it. Your potential is worth the effort of overcoming its enemies.

∞ GET MOVING ∞

God helps those who help themselves. This familiar saying expresses an important truth. Paul told Timothy to seek the help of the Holy

Spirit (see 2 Timothy 1:14), not to expect Him to run the whole show. The Holy Spirit will not take over our lives, but He will assist *us* in running them. That's the meaning of His name (*paracletus*). He is our helper or assistant. He doesn't guard our potential. He helps *us* to do so by guiding our decisions and by empowering us to withstand and triumph in the midst of trials.

Guidance, by definition, requires movement. Merriam Webster's 10th Collegiate Dictionary says that to guide is to "direct in a course or to show the way to be followed. [It] implies knowledge of the way and of all its difficulties and dangers." As a ship that is resting in the harbor cannot be steered, so the Holy Spirit cannot guide us if we are not going anywhere. When we say, "Guide me, Lord," the Holy Spirit replies, "Where are you going?" He needs us to move so He can turn us in the right direction.

If you want God to guard your potential, you have to start using it. If you want Him to protect it, you have to start protecting it. Let's say, for example, that you have a dream to go back to school and become a teacher, but you're struggling with your dream because you have poor reading skills. God will help you protect your dream of becoming a teacher if you sign up for an adult reading class and work hard to learn to read.

Or again, you may have the ambition to be a nurse or a cabinet maker or a store manager. Research the nursing programs in your area and get all the facts before you present the idea to your parents or your spouse. Find a skilled carpenter to serve under as an apprentice before you set up your own shop. Start going to school in the evenings to get your master's degree in business administration before you apply for a supervisory position. That first step you take may not be the right one, but God can't help you until you do something. He can't close a door you haven't opened or affirm a decision you haven't made. *If you aren't doing anything to accomplish your goal, He isn't doing anything either. The Holy Spirit can't work for you unless you are working.*

The same principle is true for protecting your potential. Perhaps you have the ambition to graduate from school with honors, but too much of your study time is being spent working a part-time job or hanging out with friends. Quit your job or rearrange your hours to give you more study time. Limit your social activities and make your free hours productive and relaxing. When you do something to remove the attack against your vision, God will aid your efforts. Nevertheless, *the initiative must come from you.*

Or perhaps you'd like to lose weight because your appearance is affecting both your self-esteem and the confidence others have in your ability to accomplish a given task. You know you can do the job, but you never get the chance to try because neither you nor your boss is willing to risk giving you the extra responsibility. When you make a sincere effort to watch what you eat and to get the proper exercise, God will reaffirm His estimation of your value and motivate others to see you as a capable, valuable person. His action to protect your potential depends on your actions.

God won't take a bad habit or an inappropriate lifestyle from you because He didn't give it to you. He *will* affirm your decisions and strengthen your efforts when you start taking positive steps to *rid yourself* of the negative influences, the wrong attitudes, or the poor choices that are threatening your potential. Destroy the cigarettes or drugs. Move out from living with your boyfriend or girlfriend. Stay home instead of spending every night at the local bar. Leave the room when you are about to hit your child in anger. Take responsibility for your own actions when your boss asks you why a project isn't completed or your spouse is disappointed that you forgot her birthday or your wedding anniversary.

A boat that is still cannot be turned no matter how long or how far you turn the wheel. Move a small distance and the boat will respond to a gentle touch on the wheel. The guarding and protecting of your potential is the same. If you stay stuck in your present rut with no attempts to get out of it, your dreams will wither and die. *Start moving and the gentle touch of God will begin changing you and helping you to achieve seemingly impossible dreams. God is your partner.* You must work together to protect your potential. When you start contributing to your own protection, the Holy Spirit starts to protect you as well. He empowers what you begin and redirects your efforts when they don't match His expectations. Then you can begin to discover your potential and to protect what you see.

Guarding potential is a daily task that requires more wisdom and power than we possess. God is in the business of maximizing potential. He'll empower our efforts if we cooperate with Him, but He will not do the work for us. Begin today to follow the guidelines for guarding and protecting your potential. The future of your dreams and visions is at stake.

∽ PRINCIPLES ∽

1. You are responsible to guard and protect your potential.

2. The treasure you must defend is God's wisdom, God's power, and the presence of God's Spirit in your life. This potency of God within you is your potential.

3. **Guidelines for safeguarding your potential:**
   - Recognize your enemies as the forces of evil.
   - Expect satan's attack.
   - Prepare to overcome his attack.
   - Stand firm in **the midst of attack.**

4. **Guidelines for protecting yourself from attack:**
   - Don't answer your critics.
   - Post a guard to deter attack and to warn of impending danger.
   - Allow God to fight for you.
   - Don't allow a lull in the battle to convince you that the war is over.
   - Stay away from your opposition.
   - Don't waste time talking.
   - Refuse to be intimidated by your critics' threats and accusations.

CHAPTER FIVE

CULTIVATE AND FEED YOUR POTENTIAL

Whatever you eat eventually eats you.

The old woman smiled as she entered the small, hot room. A blaze of color met her eyes. African violets of many shades of pink, purple, white, red, and blue, and variegated mixtures of these colors, filled the room. The room had not always looked like this. When she and her husband had first built this house many years before, this had been their children's playroom. Then, toys had filled the shelves.

After the last of their children had left home, the woman had become very depressed, missing the children and having very little to do. That's when a friend had given her clippings from her African violets and had persuaded her to turn the playroom into a greenhouse. The idea had been a good one, giving her renewed interest in life.

Over the years, she had spent many hours here. At first only one of the many shelves had contained plants. Now the original shelves were completely filled and others had been added. She still remembered her joy when her violets bloomed for the first time. Many hours had preceded that triumph, for she had never been known for having a green thumb. In fact, some of her friends had tried to discourage her new adventure because in the past plants had been more likely to wither than flourish while in her care. Still she had forged ahead. In time she had come to understand that her plants had failed because she had not given them sufficient care. Indeed, they had died from neglect.

When the first plants not only lived but flourished under her touch, she gained the confidence to add other colors by getting more clippings from her friend. She also began reading books and magazine articles about the care of African violets and talking with others who loved plants. One day while reading a horticulture magazine, she discovered an article on creating hybrids. That was the day she became hooked.

Since then, she had spent part of every day in this room, watering her plants, checking for insect pests, rooting new cuttings, fertilizing the plants that were about to bloom, picking off old blossoms, and rotating the plants so each one received sufficient light. Even the day her husband had died, she had wandered in here to find solace among her friends—as she had come to think of her plants.

In the evening, she often read gardening and horticulture magazines here, having moved her favorite chair from the living room when her husband was no longer there to spend the long hours with her. After nearly 40 years of hard work and extensive reading, the riotous color that surrounded her revealed the success of her efforts.

Now, her skill in cultivating and breeding African violets was known throughout the community, and over the years she had found great joy in teaching others the art of cultivating plants. Every year her conservatory was considered to be the highlight of the garden tour. Plant collections throughout the town—in gardens and rooms—were testimony to her skill.

The successful fulfillment of your potential is similar to the task of growing prizewinning flowers. Both require careful attention and diligent effort to produce winning results.

∾ Potential Doesn't Guarantee Performance ∾

God made everything with the ability to produce fruit or to reproduce itself. Yet, the potential to produce does not guarantee performance, nor does the quantity of fruit guarantee its quality. You may have a good idea that produces mediocrity-laden results. Or you may have big dreams that amount to very little. This is true because pregnancy is no guarantee of fruitfulness, and performance is not ensured by plans and dreams. Pregnancy and performance match when the potential to produce is properly cared for and developed.

Pregnancy is no guarantee of fruitfulness, and performance is not ensured by plans and dreams.

You may have the potential to be a world-class architect, but your ability does not guarantee that you will reach this level of success. You may never progress beyond drawing doll house plans for your daughter or designing a model train layout for your son. An important key to producing what you are capable of is spending the necessary time and effort to promote the development of your talent. *You must cultivate and feed your potential.*

∽ A GARDEN TO CARE FOR ∽

When God made man, shrubs had not yet appeared on the earth and plants had not yet sprung from the ground. Only after man's creation did God plant a garden and give it a river to water it. Why? Until then "there was no man to work the ground" (Genesis 2:5). The earth was pregnant but nothing was coming out because there was no one to care for the soil's babies.

Thus, we see that God created all life to depend on cultivation to maximize its existence because potential cannot be released without work. In essence, God said, "I can't allow these trees and plants to grow yet because they need cultivation when they start growing and there is no one to care for them." The fruit and seeds of many plants and trees were present in the ground, but the soil did not produce them until Adam cultivated the garden.

The New International Version of the Bible says that God gave Adam the responsibility of *working* the garden. The Revised Standard Version and the King James Version describe man's task as that of *tilling* the garden, and the Good News Bible speaks of *cultivating*. All point to man's assignment to help the garden produce to its fullest capacity. Thus, man was created to have a cultivating ministry by making the earth grow richer as he gives to it, feeds it, and adds to it.

∽ WINNING THE PRIZE REQUIRES RUNNING THE RACE ∽

Potential is like soil. It must be worked and fed to produce fruit. King Solomon referred to this process of releasing the fruitfulness of man when he said, "The purposes of a man's heart are deep waters, but a man of understanding draws them out" (Proverbs 20:5).

Notice, the drawing out of man's potential requires effort. Like the fisherman who brings forth the treasures of the sea by hard work and the farmer who harvests the fruit of the ground by the sweat of his brow, so man must labor to tap even a portion of God's potential within him.

Potential is like soil.
It must be worked and fed to produce fruit.

The apostle Paul understood this need to put forth the effort to release his fruitfulness.

Do you not know that in a race all the runners run, but only one gets the prize? Run in such a way as to get the prize. Everyone who competes in the games goes into strict training. They do it to get a crown that will not last; but we do it to get a crown that will last forever. Therefore I do not run like a man running aimlessly; I do not fight like a man beating the air. No, I beat my body and make it my slave so that after I have preached to others, I myself will not be disqualified for the prize (1 Corinthians 9:24-27).

Understanding and wisdom are the keys to the success of man's mission. His race to maximize everything God has given him begins with knowing what God requires of him and how He expects him to reach the finish line. The primary principle in cultivating one's life for maximum living is to destroy ignorance by the pursuit of knowledge, wisdom, and understanding.

KNOWLEDGE AND UNDERSTANDING PROMOTE GROWTH

Suppose I wanted to create a beautiful vase to place in my living room, but I knew nothing about making pottery. My first step would need to be a visit to a master potter, or at least to the local library, to learn all I could about working clay into beautiful pieces. I would have to learn about the selection and preparation of the clay, the throwing and shaping of the vase on the potter's wheel, the length of time and the conditions for seasoning the raw pot, the proper temperature and duration for firing the pot in the kiln, etc. Much work, including many hours of practice on much lesser pots than the vase I hoped to create, would precede my reaching the goal of making a vase to place in my living room.

This procedure is not unlike the process we must undertake to maximize our potential. Knowledge and effort must co-exist, but knowledge is the foundation for success. As we saw in the last chapter, God's wisdom and knowledge become available to us when we are connected to Him through the presence of His Spirit. An understanding of His ways and the discovery of His purposes are part of the treasure He has given us.

For the Lord gives wisdom, and from His mouth come knowledge and understanding. He holds victory in store for the upright, He is a shield to those whose walk is blameless, for He guards the course of the just and protects the way of His faithful ones. Then you will understand what is right and just and fair—every good path. For wisdom will enter your heart, and knowledge will be pleasant to your soul (Proverbs 2:6-10).

The search for knowledge requires effort. You must seek it like a treasure that is precious to you. You cannot touch God's knowledge, however, without diligence and exertion.

Apply your heart to instruction and your ears to words of knowledge (Proverbs 23:12).

My son, if you accept my words and store up my commands within you, turning your ear to wisdom and applying your heart to understanding, and if you call out for insight and cry aloud for understanding, and if you look for it as for silver and search for it as for hidden treasure, then you will understand the fear of the Lord and find the knowledge of God (Proverbs 2:1-5).

By wisdom a house is built, and through understanding it is established; through knowledge its rooms are filled with rare and beautiful treasures. A wise man has great power, and a man of knowledge increases strength; for waging war you need guidance, and for victory many advisers (Proverbs 24:3-6).

Building a house and waging war require great effort. They do not just happen. The same is true for storing up things. If you've ever canned or frozen fruits and vegetables in the summer to provide for your family in the winter, you know that many long, hot hours precede the final act of putting the finished jars on the shelf.

In a similar manner, removing treasures from the earth is also arduous and time-consuming. Wells must be drilled before oil can be pumped from the depths of the earth, and great shafts or tunnels must be dug before the mining of diamonds, silver, and other precious metals can be achieved. These are the images Solomon used to illustrate the strength and the dedication you will need to exercise if you hope to gain the knowledge that will advance the unleashing of your potential.

Knowledge must always precede action or much time and effort will be wasted through misguided efforts and dead-end directions. God, who planned your life and granted you the potential to fulfill

His plans, works for and with you when you seek to know Him and to understand and follow His ways.

**Knowledge must always precede action
or much time and effort will be wasted through
misguided efforts and dead-end directions.**

∾ THE CONSEQUENCES OF NEGLECTING KNOWLEDGE ∾

Sadly, we often forfeit our potential because we neglect the wisdom, knowledge, and understanding that come from God alone. Solomon spoke of the consequences of this neglect, as did the prophet Hosea:

Wise men store up knowledge, but the mouth of a fool invites ruin (Proverbs 10:14).

The teaching of the wise is a fountain of life, turning a man from the snares of death. Good understanding wins favor, but the way of the unfaithful is hard. Every prudent man acts out of knowledge, but a fool exposes his folly (Proverbs 13:14-16).

My people are destroyed from lack of knowledge. "Because you have rejected knowledge, I also reject you as My priests; because you have ignored the law of your God, I also will ignore your children" (Hosea 4:6).

A lack of knowledge is not the same as the unavailability of knowledge. Hosea says that God's people perish because they have *rejected* knowledge. Knowledge may surround us, but unless we apply it to our situation or use it to inform our decisions, it is useless to us. We cannot really excuse ourselves before the Lord saying, "I didn't know," because opportunities to gain knowledge abound in our world. We live in an age of an information explosion with libraries, tape ministries, teaching videos, television, and radio bombarding us on every side with opportunities to stretch our horizons and increase our knowledge. What we can confess to God is, "I rejected the opportunity to learn."

The saying, "What you don't know can't kill you," is simply not true. Too often we suffer loss because we did not take the opportunity to learn the facts about a particular subject. We perish because of what we don't know. *No matter how great your dream is, if you don't have the information relative to your plan, forget it.*

∞ THE PENALTIES OF IGNORANCE ∞

The devil doesn't destroy God's people...the government doesn't destroy God's people...the economy doesn't destroy God's people...cocaine and marijuana don't destroy God's people. *Ignorance* destroys God's people. This one thing is behind every destructive influence in our lives.

God rejects those who reject His knowledge. In other words He says, "We can't do business. You haven't used the tools I gave you, so I can't help you. You can't even talk intelligently with Me." Ignorance affects how God answers our prayers because we ask for things we don't need or shouldn't want. To ask rightly we must understand how we operate, how the devil operates, how the world operates, and how God operates. Asking God to do something for us before we understand these aspects of our situation is wasting our time and God's. He must reject everything we request because our prayers and His ways, will, and desires for us do not line up.

Ignorance affects how God answers our prayers because we ask for things we don't need or shouldn't want.

Research your dream before you start working to achieve it. Learn everything you can about the business you want to start or the people you want to reach. You need good information to make right decisions.

God also ignores the children of those who ignore His knowledge. This is true because your children learn what you know. If you don't know anything, they aren't going to learn anything, and they will thus make the same mistakes and have the same values and attitudes you have.

Ignorance messes up the next generation. It destroys not only your fruitfulness but your children's as well. Thus, you and your children reap what you sow, and *your* lack of information harms *them*. Our world is experiencing a multitude of human disasters that give evidence to this fact. Abortion, AIDS, environmental issues, drugs—all reveal the consequences of the rejection of knowledge by this generation and those that preceded us. In essence, ignorance is generational and transferable. The decision to pursue knowledge, improve understanding, and gain wisdom is a personal decision but not a private issue. Every book you read affects your grandchildren, so read and cultivate yourself for posterity.

∽ TWISTED VALUES ∽

Our ignorance of God's will and His ways has twisted our world. We devalue what God values and elevate what is insignificant to Him. He sees the tremendous ability we have and we look at the earth houses that contain that treasure (see 2 Corinthians 4:7). He created us to show forth His power, but we are more interested in success by the world's standards. He affirms our ability to tap into His wisdom, but we make decisions based on the information we receive from our physical senses and our education.

Our poverty of knowledge is revealed by our inability to fulfill God's potential on our own. We live aimlessly without purpose, flitting from one thing to another and never accomplishing anything. Such life is a waste of time. Without a sense of purpose we are like stillborn babies.

Your potential will be wasted if you do not allow God to cleanse your sight and redirect your values. Then you can escape this purposeless existence. This occurs as you become aware of the world's standards and compare them carefully with God's. You may be surprised by what you find.

POTENTIAL UNDER ATTACK

The Bible says, "Man looks at the outward appearance, but the Lord looks at the heart" (1 Samuel 16:7c). It's time you and I reevaluate the standards of the world. Our cars are faster but weaker. Our clothes are sharper, but they come apart at the seams. Our vinyl shoes shine nicely, but they lack the durability of leather. What appears to be better may indeed be a compromise on value and worth. These upside-down values are attacking your potential.

Our world has become very concerned about pollution issues. Environmental groups are angered by oil spills and they warn us about the need to protect endangered animals, rain forests, and waterways. As consumers we are constantly reminded to dispose of waste properly as part of the effort to protect our planet's air and water supplies, and we are encouraged to recycle to promote the wise use of the earth's resources.

Sadly, we are more concerned about the destruction of the earth's atmosphere than we are about the poisoning of our children by the airwaves they breathe in our homes. We are interested in the purity of the water we drink, but we do not monitor the pollutants that fill our minds. Our world is sick because we value the wrong things.

In the Gospel of Mark, Jesus rebuked the Pharisees because their values were mixed up. As Jesus and His disciples were walking through a grain field, they were picking and eating grain because they were hungry. Since it was the Sabbath, the Pharisees complained that they were breaking the law.

He answered [them], *"Have you never read what David did when he and his companions were hungry and in need?...he entered the house of God and ate the consecrated bread, which is lawful only for priests to eat. And he also gave some to his companions." Then He said to them, "The Sabbath was made for man, not man for the Sabbath. So the Son of Man is Lord even of the Sabbath."*

Another time [Jesus] *went into the synagogue, and a man with a shriveled hand was there. Some of* [the Pharisees] *were looking for a reason to accuse Jesus, so they watched Him closely to see if He would heal him on the Sabbath. Jesus said to the man with the shriveled hand, "Stand up in front of everyone." Then Jesus asked them, "Which is lawful on the Sabbath: to do good or to do evil, to save life or to kill?" But they remained silent. He looked around at them in anger and, deeply distressed at their stubborn hearts, said to the man, "Stretch out your hand." He stretched it out, and his hand was completely restored* (Mark 2:25–3:5).

Matthew records Jesus' words on this occasion slightly differently:

[Jesus] *said to them, "If any of you has a sheep and it falls into a pit on the Sabbath, will you not take hold of it and lift it out? How much more valuable is a man than a sheep! Therefore it is lawful to do good on the Sabbath"* (Matthew 12:11-12).

The values and standards of our world are not so different from those of the Pharisees. We save whales and try to protect endangered species, but we allow babies to be aborted. We cannot shoot flamingos, but we can take a scalpel and kill human fetuses.

We are sick. We are no different than those Jesus admonished. Therefore, we need to rethink our values and redefine the definition of pollution. *The most damaging pollutants that are poisoning our communities are not coming from cars, factories, and toxic waste dumps. They come from bookshelves, televisions, movie houses, and rental videos.* They come from our schools and colleges where teachers who do not believe in God teach our children that God is a crutch or a figment of their imaginations. Don't tell me not to shoot flamingos when teachers are shooting my children by teaching them corruption, error, evolution, and Godless philosophies!

The only way to combat this pollution is to examine what we are feeding our children and to cultivate with care the environments in which they grow. Then we can activate and stimulate their potential, and ours, with the proper nutrients and fertilizers. God determined this need to care for our potential when He placed Adam in the garden and commanded him to work, till, and cultivate it.

∞ A TWOFOLD PROCESS: CULTIVATING AND FEEDING YOUR POTENTIAL ∞

Potential must be cultivated and fed to produce fruit. But how do we do this? How do we cultivate and feed the talents, skills, and abilities we possess?

The definitions of *cultivate* include: a) to prepare and work to promote growth; b) to improve growth by labor and attention; c) to develop and refine by education and training; and d) to seek or promote, such as a friendship. To *feed* something means that we a) supply with nourishment; b) provide as food; c) furnish for consumption; and d) satisfy, minister, and gratify. All these definitions imply that the process is to be beneficial, not harmful. If the provisions do not supply nourishment that is essential for growth, they are not truly feeding us. Likewise, if the activity and attention do not help us to develop, refine, improve, and promote our abilities, skills, and talents, they cannot truly be called cultivation.

Even as seeds do not become plants overnight, so the wealth of our potential cannot be exposed and fulfilled in an instant. We must exert effort to cultivate what God has given us, and we must exercise care to fertilize and water it properly. As specific plants require certain nutrients and conditions to grow, so we must provide the right nourishment and environment to encourage the maximizing of our potential. These specifications have been set by God, who created us. To ignore them is to invite death.

Cultivating and Feeding the Three Dimensions of Potential

We are like a fallow field. We contain much fruit, but our fertility will not become evident until and unless we cultivate and feed our bodies, souls, and spirits. These are the three dimensions of potential. Cultivating and feeding work together to promote maximum growth and fulfillment. If we activate and stimulate our potential through challenging work and experiences, but we neglect to provide the appropriate fertilizers that will sustain and maintain it within those situations, before long growth will become stunted and eventually stop. Likewise, if we feed our bodies, souls, and spirits according to our Manufacturer's specifications, but we fail to foster and develop occasions when we can try new things and reach for new goals, we will still diminish the effective release of our potential. Both cultivating and feeding are necessary for wholesome growth.

Each dimension of our potential—body, soul, and spirit—has definite specifications and materials for cultivation and explicit requirements in fertilizers. These specifications or requirements prescribed by our Manufacturer ensure that each part of our being operates at peak performance and achieves maximum fruitfulness. They are essential ingredients for unveiling who we can be and what we can do.

You are what you eat. This is true for all three dimensions of potential. If you eat excessive fatty foods, you will gain weight and your face will be covered with pimples. If you feed your mind with trash, your thoughts will be in the gutter. If you feed your spirit the information received through the senses of your body and the education of your soul, neglecting God's wisdom and knowledge, you will operate from worldly standards and values.

You are what you eat.

Cultivate and Feed Your Body

Your body is a precise machine that requires proper food, exercise, and rest. Healthy food, regular exercise, and scheduled periods of rest are essential for it to operate at its maximum potential. Physical health deteriorates when sweets, fats, or other harmful foods are stuffed into the body, and the body's strength and endurance are lessened if exercise (work) is missing from your daily routine. Likewise, the absence of rest depletes the body's resources until exhaustion and even collapse eventually occur. Cultivate and feed your body by living within a healthy routine that includes nutritious food, moderate but systematic exercise, and regular sleep and relaxation.

Secondly, the cultivation and feeding of your body requires that you use it with discretion, setting it apart for its intended uses. God did not give you a physical body so you can fill it with empty calories or treat it as a beast of burden. If you have a choice of a salad or french fries for lunch, choose the salad. The fries may taste good, but they do little or nothing to nourish you. In a similar manner, consider the proper use of your body when you are working or exercising. For example, safeguard your back by bending your knees to lift a heavy load.

This requirement to use your body with discretion also means that you should treat it with respect and exercise caution not to abuse it. Take care not to allow cigarettes, alcohol, and other harmful substances to enter it. As the apostle Paul warns us:

For we must all appear before the judgment seat of Christ, that each one may receive what is due him for the things done while in the body, whether good or bad (2 Corinthians 5:10).

Each person will have to give an account for what he did with his body.

Third, you must cultivate your physical body by preserving it and protecting it from pollutants. If you are going to do something for the world, if you are really going to contribute to the effectiveness and the productivity of your nation, you cannot be sick because you cannot be effective if you are sick. As the apostle Paul says:

Do you not know that your body is a temple of the Holy Spirit, who is in you, whom you have received from God? ...Therefore honor God with your body (1 Corinthians 6:19-20).

In his letter to the church at Rome, Paul adds:

...offer your bodies as living sacrifices, holy and pleasing to God— this is your spiritual act of worship (Romans 12:1).

For something to be a sacrifice, it must be valuable and worth giving. You cannot effectively honor God if your body is too heavy or your heart is weak because you have filled your body with cholesterol-producing foods. Preserve your body by understanding and obeying the Manufacturer's directions. You are responsible to protect your physical temple. Cultivate your body.

Cultivate Your Soul

Your soul consists of your mind, your will, and your emotions. *What goes into your mind always influences what comes out.* If your children watch disrespectful, smart-mouthed kids on TV, they will learn to talk and act the same way. In fact, they won't even know that they are being disrespectful because their values and wisdom will have been skewed by the things they saw and read.

Be careful, then, to *convert your mind* by filling it with godly, uplifting materials. Feed it God's Word instead of junk novels. If you spend much time reading ivory-towered romantic fiction, you will come to have unrealistic expectations of your spouse and you will either degrade or destroy the marriage relationship through unfaithful thoughts, words, and actions. Turn on a teaching tape instead of the afternoon soaps. Take part in a small group Bible study. Use your moments of leisure to uplift rather than tear down.

Likewise, *cultivate your mind.* Spend some time each week in serious Bible study or research a useful topic you know little about at your local library. Attend concerts and lectures, or take evening classes at a community college. The whole purpose of encyclopedias, formal education, and other sources of knowledge is not to make you smart, but to give you the opportunity to make yourself smart. Use the resources available to your mind to inspire you to activate your dreams and reach for new goals. Your mind is a powerful tool created by God for the good of mankind.

It's a pity to die with water when people are dying of thirst. Yet it happens every day as people who have the answers to the world's problems refuse to feed and cultivate their minds so they can reach into the deep wells of their possibilities and pull out what the world needs. Look to the careful cultivation and feeding of your mind. Remember, the person who *doesn't* read is no better off than the person who *can't.*

**It's a pity to die with water
when people are dying of thirst.**

The cultivation of your soul also includes the discipline of your will. Discipline is training or teaching someone or something to obey a particular command or to live by a certain standard. The discipline of your will is particularly important because the will is the decision maker. If you refuse to discipline your will, you won't be successful in fulfilling your potential because *your will determines your decisions, which govern your potential.*

I imagine Jesus in the garden before His arrest. His will was saying, "Let's find another way to do this," but God said, "There is only one way." Because Jesus' will was disciplined, He said, "Okay, Your will not Mine be done." (See Mark 14:32-36.) If you do not train your will to be subjected to God's wisdom and purposes, you will forfeit the purpose for which you were born, and your potential will be wasted. Self-discipline is the highest expression of self-management, which is manifested in a disciplined will.

The cultivating of your soul also requires that you control your emotions. Too often we allow our emotions to control us instead of our controlling them. Tantrums and fits of rage are symptoms of this malady. Emotions are controlled by understanding. Ecclesiastes 7:12 says:

Wisdom is a shelter as money is a shelter, but the advantage of knowledge is this: that wisdom preserves the life of its possessor.

What we know to be true from seeking information and examining the facts must be the basis on which we make decisions and relate to other people. Emotions often color what we see. They also prompt us to say hasty words and to make unwise choices. Emotions governed by information provides an environment in which the potential of our souls can be maximized.

Better a patient man than a warrior, a man who controls his temper than one who takes a city (Proverbs 16:32).

Jesus said that *the soul is the most important dimension of our make-up because the soul is both our receiving center and our distribution center*. It receives information through our physical senses and discernment through our spirits and it sends directions back to both our bodies and our spirits. Thus, our souls processes information from both the physical and the spiritual worlds. Jesus said in Matthew 5:5, "Blessed are the meek, for they will inherit the earth." The word *meek* does not mean "weak," but rather "controlled power" or "disciplined energy." Self-discipline will cause God to trust us to manage more of the earth's resources.

Too often the soul is neglected and permitted to pick up information that is not good for the spirit. Maximize your potential by cultivating and feeding your soul so that your spirit may fellowship with God, who is the source of all potential.

Cultivate and Feed Your Spirit

Maximizing your potential begins with your decision to accept Jesus Christ as your Lord and Savior because the measure of your true potential is your spirit. Until you become reconnected with God through faith in Jesus Christ and the presence of His Spirit in your heart, you are spiritually dead, and the potential of your spirit is unavailable to you. Then your mind can only be controlled by what you receive through your senses and your mind.

Those who live according to the sinful nature have their minds set on what that nature desires; but those who live in accordance with the Spirit have their minds set on what the Spirit desires. The mind of sinful man is death, but the mind controlled by the Spirit is life and peace (Romans 8:5-6).

The secret wisdom of God concerning your potential (see 1 Corinthians 2:7-11) cannot influence your life if His Spirit is not

present in your heart because only God's Spirit knows and understands God's plans and purposes for you. These were written long
before your birth. They contain the information you need to live to
the fullest and to achieve everything you were sent to do. Attaining
your maximum potential is impossible if you do not cultivate and
feed your spirit by hooking yourself up to God and abiding in Him.
(See John 15:1-8.)

Cultivating and feeding your potential is a second key to maximizing your potential. As you pay attention to the fertilizer you
give your body, soul, and spirit, and the work you do to keep them
healthy by the Manufacturer's specifications, you will be surprised
and delighted by the many things you can accomplish and the satisfaction and joy in life you will experience. *You must cultivate and
feed your potential according to God's specifications and with His
materials.*

**Show me your friends,
and I will show you your future.**

∞ PRINCIPLES ∞

**1. The potential to produce fruit does not guarantee either
fruitfulness or the quality of the fruit.**

**2. Potential must be worked (cultivated) and fed to pro-
duce fruit.**

**3. Ignorance messes up the next generation because God
rejects both those who reject knowledge, and their children.**

4. God designed the potential of your body, your soul, and your spirit to be maximized by specific fertilizers and environments that promote positive growth and development.

5. Cultivate and feed your body by getting the proper food, exercise, and rest, by using it with discretion, and by preserving and protecting it from pollutants.

6. Cultivate and feed your soul by feeding your mind positive, Godly information, by disciplining your will to discover and live by God's wisdom and purposes, and by governing your emotions with God's truth.

7. Cultivate and feed your spirit by living from God's secret wisdom dispensed through His Holy Spirit.

CHAPTER SIX

SHARE YOUR POTENTIAL

Giving is the greatest evidence of true freedom. It is more productive to give than receive (see Acts 20:35).

Silently the orchestra waited. What would this new masterpiece of their beloved conductor be like? He had promised that it would be different from anything he had ever written. As each player received his part, he looked at it in surprise. Although each score contained some notes, there were many more rests than notes. All assumed the other instruments must have the lead part for the piece.

When they started to play, however, it soon became evident that no one had the lead. The trumpets would play for a few measures, then the trombones, after which the clarinets or the flutes picked up the tune. Although it was true that the parts had some resemblance to each other, no clear melody was evident. The longer the musicians played, the stranger the music became, but they kept playing because it seemed to be what the conductor expected.

After five minutes of each instrument playing a few notes here and there, the conductor laid down his baton and looked at the musicians. "What is wrong?" he asked. "Don't you like the music?"

Quickly the members of the orchestra looked at each other. What should they say? No, they did not like the piece, for it had none of the beauty and grandeur they had come to expect in the maestro's music. Rather than hurt their leader's feelings, they said nothing.

Then the maestro started to laugh. "Wait," he said, "I will be right back." When he returned, his arms were again filled with music. Once more he moved through the orchestra, giving each player a score. This time when he lifted his baton, anticipation filled each face. Although the scores still contained rests, they were considerably fewer and they seemed to be at fitting places.

After the orchestra had played for a few minutes, the conductor stopped them and asked, "Do you understand what I have done? If you look at the notes on the two scores, you will notice that they are the same. It is the rests that are different. The first time, one of you played a little, then another, then a third player. You never played together. I did this to show you that each part is important, but it is meaningless without the others. When we all play the right notes at the right time, blending the music and sharing the unique sounds of each instrument, a beautiful melody emerges. Unlike the strange awkwardness of the first score, the second score highlights each instrument at the appropriate time, with the other instruments playing the supporting chords and the countermelodies. This is the way music is supposed to sound."

∽ SHARING MAXIMIZES AND FULFILLS POTENTIAL ∽

This blending and support is also the way potential is meant to be used. Even as the beauty of a symphony is minimized when each instrument's part is played in isolation, so the wealth of our potential is minimized when we do not share it with others Potential is maximized and fulfilled only when it is shared. This sharing of potential is God's way of bringing to pass His plans and purposes for men and women.

The wealth of our potential is minimized when we do not share it with others.

GOD SHARES HIS POTENTIAL

God's nature is built around sharing and giving. Before the world was created, everything existed in Him. All that we have seen, now see, and yet will see comes from Him. God could have kept all this stuff inside Him, but it wouldn't have benefited Him there. He had to release it through creativity before the beauty and power of His potential could be revealed.

Everything God called into being He gave a purpose that meshes with the larger purpose of the world. Every animal, bird, fish, insect, reptile, plant, and tree is connected to the whole of creation. If one species becomes extinct, its death disrupts and impacts the entire eco-system. In essence, each part of God's world in some way balances and enriches the rest.

YOU SHARE GOD'S POTENTIAL

Human beings are God's crowning creative act. The treasure He put in us He took from Himself. He chose to give us part of His potential so we could use it for Him. God could have run the world by Himself, but He brought us into His plan so we could bring glory to Him by revealing all He is. He doesn't need our involvement to accomplish all He is capable of doing and being, but He wants us to enjoy the blessing of participating in His purpose. *Your gifts, talents, and abilities are your share of the endowment God gives to mankind to bless all creation.*

As a parent enjoys watching a child learn new things, God finds satisfaction in watching you discover and use your potential. In essence, you show forth God's nature and reveal His potency when you fulfill your potential *Your purpose is equal to your potential, and your potential is equal to your purpose.* The more you understand your purpose, the more you will discover what you can do.

God finds satisfaction in watching you discover and use your potential.

Thus, God gets excited when you take authority over your bad habits. He enjoys watching you discover and use the deposit of His power and wisdom within you. Sometimes it would be easier for God to just snap His fingers and take over, but then He'd lose the joy of watching you order your life and the pleasure of seeing you expose His potential.

The other day, my wife and I were sitting at the table where our little girl was doing her homework. She had to spell some words and find the words that rhymed. I was so tempted to give her all the answers because I knew them right away. I held back because I knew I would rob her of the pleasure of producing her own potential.

God works with you in the same way. There are some things He'd like to do for you, but He's holding back so you can enjoy your success when you do them yourself. You say, "God, change this situation," and God responds, "Well, I could, but there's something you could learn about what you are capable of doing and being, so no, I won't take over and do it for you."

Just as I tell my daughter, "You figure it out," when she asks me, "Daddy, what's this?" so God allows you to work things out for yourself. He's proud of you when you succeed, just like I'm proud of my daughter when she successfully completes her homework. I produced her as part of my responsibility, now I find pleasure in seeing her use what I shared with her.

God finds the same pleasure in you. He has shared His potential with you, now He wants to enjoy the benefits of that gift. His joy overflows when you release all He has given you.

❧ POTENTIAL IS NEVER GIVEN FOR ITSELF ❧

When I was in college, I went on a tour of Europe. After several days, I lost interest in all I was seeing because my fiancée, who is now my wife, was not there to share it with me. On that trip I learned the truth of this principle: *Potential is never given for itself. Whatever God gives to you, He gives for others.*

Even as a solitary instrument cannot produce the majestic music of a symphonic orchestra, so human beings cannot glorify their Creator in isolation. I need your potential to maximize mine, and you need my potential to maximize yours. All we have been given is meant to be shared.

ISOLATION IS NOT GOOD

After man had finished naming all the animals and no suitable helper for him was found among them, God performed another significant act of creation. Why? "It is not good for the man to be alone" (Genesis 2:18).

God did not make woman because man asked for a wife, nor because a helper for man was a good idea. Man *needed* a companion because he could not realize his potential without sharing it with someone. His solitary existence was not good.

To be solitary or alone is not the same as being single. To be alone is to be isolated and cut off from others. Communication is impossible because you have no one like yourself to share with. This is what God says is not good.

To be single is to be unmarried. Marriage is not a requirement or a prerequisite for the fulfillment of your potential. You do not necessarily *need* a husband or a wife. What you do need, however, is someone with whom you can share your potential. This is true because *your personal satisfaction is connected to your fulfilling God's purpose for your life, and your purpose cannot be achieved in isolation.* You need those people who will call forth your potential and into whom you can pour your life. *You may be wired to be single, but you are not designed to live isolated and alone.*

You need someone with whom you can share your potential.

A WORD OF CAUTION

You must be careful, however, when, how, and with whom you share your potential. Even as isolation is not good for personal fulfillment and the maximizing of potential, so sharing your hidden wealth in a manner that transgresses God's laws of limitation is not good. All your natural abilities, all the gifts you have cultivated, and all the knowledge you have accumulated are yours to share within the context of God's principles, plans, and purposes. *God created everything to fulfill its potential within the limitations of certain laws.* In other words, He specified the boundaries within which all things can perform to their maximum capabilities.

For example, God created you to serve only Him. The context of living in an obedient relationship with Him is the only means of ensuring your happiness and fulfillment. Therefore, God commands you:

You shall have no other gods before Me. You shall not make for yourself an idol.... You shall not bow down to them or worship them (Exodus 20:3-5a).

His command seeks to safeguard your ideal environment because He knows that you cannot satisfy your spiritual potential if you worship or bow down to something or someone else.

In a similar manner, *God set a physical context within which your potential may be shared. This physical context is the relationship originally enjoyed by Adam and Eve when Eve was given to Adam to be his helpmeet.* This God-given requirement for sharing physical potential is made visible in His command: "Be fruitful and increase in number; fill the earth and subdue it" (Genesis 1:28).

Neither two males nor two females can produce a baby because man's potential is fulfilled by sharing it with a woman, and woman's is fulfilled by sharing it with a man. For their potential to be fruitful, men and women must share their physical potential within the context of a male-female relationship that is within the bonds of marriage.

What is known today as an alternative lifestyle is truly the abuse of natural destiny and the violation of human nature because it prevents this fulfillment of purpose. Woman was created to receive, and man was created to give. Thus, their shared potentials complement each other. A man cannot be fruitful without a woman, nor can a woman be fruitful without a man. Two givers or two receivers cannot work together to produce fruit. Be careful that you share your physical potential with the right person.

Your soulical potential is fulfilled by sharing it within the context of the family. Here a child learns to give and receive love and affection. Very often psychological and emotional problems arise when love is not felt and expressed in the formative years. If a boy never feels loved by his mother, he may become confused later in life if a male starts meeting some of those needs. Then his ability to give and receive affection, affirmation, and attention seeks to be fulfilled in the wrong context.

Men can enjoy deep and lasting friendships with men, but they must be careful what they share within that relationship. Certain things are good to share; others are not. The same is true of friendships between women. God intends that you will fulfill your basic soulical potential within the context of the family.

⁓ POTENTIAL IS FULFILLED WHEN IT IS RELEASED ⁓

Potential is fulfilled only when it is given to others. You cannot enjoy or fulfill your potential if you keep it to yourself. Everything God gave you, He gave for me and everyone else. He blesses you with additional gifts when you use the blessings you have already received to bless others. In other words, *fruitfulness is always given to make you a blessing to others. You are blessed when you take what you have and give it away.* This is true because sharing your potential both reveals hidden possibilities and releases additional gifts.

**Everything God gave you,
He gave for me and everyone else.**

A seed produces nothing if it does not surrender its potential to the soil. If it says, "I'm going to keep what I have," its potential to produce a tree is lost. Only as the seed relinquishes its outer shell and puts down roots that permit it to receive nourishment from the soil can it release its potential to be a tree. Through self-giving, the seed is transformed and gives birth to new possibilities. Then the tree, having been blessed by the gift of the seed, begins to push out blossoms, showing forth some of its fruit. In time, it yields fruit with more seed that can continue the cycle of giving. If anything along the way chooses to withhold its potential—be it the seed, the tree, or the fruit—the cycle is broken and much potential is lost.

This same truth is evident in the music of an orchestra. The instruments' potential to produce music cannot be fulfilled until the individual notes are released by the players. If even one player refuses to release what he possesses, the loss extends far beyond the one who withholds his contribution because the withheld potential of one affects the potential of all. Indeed, the music either remains hidden and dormant or it emerges misshapen and incomplete. All suffer loss—musicians and music—if even one person or one instrument refuses to cooperate. Only as all give of what they possess can the potential of the music be released.

GIVING EXPOSES POTENTIAL

Treasures that are hidden and locked up benefit no one. Say, for example, that your grandmother gave you a beautiful necklace that she wore as a bride. If you keep it locked in a safe and never wear it, its beauty is wasted.

Or perhaps you have wedding gifts of beautiful china, sterling silver, and fine crystal that you have never used to serve a meal. You're wasting the potential of those dishes. They cannot do what they are supposed to do sitting on a shelf. People bought them for you to use. *Treasure is useless unless you expose it.* Potential can never be attained if it has no opportunity to give.

> **Potential can never be attained
> if it has no opportunity to give.**

This was the power of John F. Kennedy's words, spoken at his inauguration to be the president of the United States: "Ask not what your country can do for you, but what you can do for your country." Kennedy's words prompt us to focus on what we can *give* instead of what we can *get*. It is through our giving that we discover what we can do and be.

This was also the wisdom shared by the apostle Paul, "It is more blessed to give than to receive" (Acts 20:35). Releasing what you have received benefits you and others. Holding on to a treasure forfeits the blessing inherit in the treasure, and no one profits from it. Like the seed, *you must release what God has stored in you for the world.* You do this by releasing seeds into the soil of the lives of others.

GOD IS A GIVER

God is constantly releasing seeds into the soil of your life. He is a giver and He created you to be like Him. The foundation of God's giving nature is revealed in His purpose for creating men and women.

God made Adam and Eve so He would have someone to love and bless—more children like Christ, His Incarnate Son. Although God possessed all He had created, those things were useless to Him until He created man to release their potential by using His creations and, thereby, showing off His fullness.

In essence, God, who is love, created man to fulfill His potential to love. Love is worthless until it is given away. It must have an object to be fulfilled. Therefore, God needed something on which He could lavish His love, something that could understand and appreciate what He had to give. Of all God's creatures, only men and women share God's Spirit and, thus, can appreciate His love.

You are the object of God's love. Because love can be fulfilled only when the receiver of love is like the giver, He created you like Himself, to be loved by Him and to love as He loves.

THE MUTUALITY OF GIVING

Think about the last time you bought a card or a gift for a spouse or a close friend. Much of the pleasure in giving the gift is found in choosing something that will delight the one to whom you are giving it. The gift's meaning is found in the shared love of the giver and the recipient.

This is the meaning of Jesus' words:

Do not give dogs what is sacred; do not throw your pearls to pigs. If you do, they may trample them under their feet, and then turn and tear you to pieces (Matthew 7:6).

A pet cannot appreciate a diamond ring, but your sweetheart will. Why? She understands the thoughts and the feelings that both prompted the gift and are revealed in it. The one who receives a gift must understand and appreciate the giver before the gift can have meaning. Through giving love is released.

You have been physically birthed by the giving of your parents and spiritually birthed by the giving of Christ. Even as your parents gave the seed of their bodies to release their potential to produce another human being, so Jesus Christ gave the seed that brings new life by releasing His potential to be a Savior. Their giving brings you life and the opportunity to continue the cycle of giving. Joy is found in participating in the pattern of giving, receiving, and giving again. This pattern of releasing potential by giving and receiving is particularly visible in the biblical concept of a blessing.

BLESSED TO BE A BLESSING

The giving of a blessing is an important image in Scripture. Whether it is God, a father, or some other person giving the blessing, it is a gift that exposes possibilities and releases power. God blessed Adam and Eve (see Genesis 1:28), and Noah and his sons (see Genesis 9:1), by calling forth from them the potential to be fruitful, to increase in number, and to fill the earth. Likewise, He blessed Sarah, the wife of Abraham, when He released the possibility that she would be a mother (see Genesis 17:15-16). Isaac passed the power to be the lord of the family on to Jacob when he blessed him (see Genesis 27:27-29). Jacob in turn blessed each of his sons, unveiling the future of each one (see Genesis 49). In each case, the blessing confirmed what God had already purposed for the one who received the blessing.

Blessings are never given solely for the benefit of the one who receives them. That means all God has given you—your clothes, food, house, car, bike, education, intelligence, personality, etc.—are given to you so you can maximize them by sharing them. You cannot release the full potential of anything if you do not share it.

Blessings are never given solely for the benefit of the one who receives them.

Abraham not only *received* a blessing from God; he was also *made* a blessing to others:

I will make you into a great nation and I will bless you; I will make your name great, and you will be a blessing. I will bless those who bless you, and whoever curses you I will curse; and all peoples on earth will be blessed through you (Genesis 12:2-3).

The same was true for Abraham's wife, Sarah (see Genesis 17:16), his son Isaac (see Genesis 26:4), and his grandson Jacob (see Genesis 28:14). God's blessing also worked through Jacob's son Joseph, who preserved God's people through a severe famine. Each passed on God's blessings so others could be blessed.

God operates from this perspective: "I'm going to share with you so you will be blessed by My sharing and you, in turn, will bless others by your sharing." He gives to you so you can share His potential by being motivated to pass on all He gives you. Therefore, *the task of humanity is to emulate the attitude of God by drawing from each person all he or she possesses.* You exist to pull things from me, and I exist to pull things from you.

God finds joy in giving to you so you can give to others. He blesses you to bless another. No matter what your circumstances are, there is some way you can share your potential with others. If you are homebound, give yourself through prayer or the ministry of encouragement through cards, letters, and phone calls. Or perhaps you are retired with few financial resources but much time. Pour yourself into a child.

Whatever your blessings, find some way to share them. This is God's intention for giving them to you. Your gifts may be different from mine, but their value is equal if we serve the same Lord with the same Spirit (see 1 Corinthians 12:1-7). *Your gifts are for me and my gifts are for you. Together we can bless the world.* This is how potential is released.

⊷ RECEIVING WITHOUT GIVING RESULTS IN DESTRUCTION ⊷

True joy is found not in what you accomplish but in who benefits from your success. Dying to yourself and giving for me and others will reap for you the joy of seeing your efforts reproduced many times over in us. Your sharing will give life to many.

If, however, you refuse to share, you will destroy both God's joy in giving to you and your joy in passing on what He gives. You will also forfeit His blessings because those who wish to receive from the abundance of God must use wisely all He gives. This is true because selfishness concerns itself only with its own prosperity and well-being. It lacks interest in the concerns and needs of others.

You cannot emulate the giving nature of God if you retain all you have for your own wants and needs; neither can your bucket draw from the deep waters in me. Such selfishness kills potential and lessens the likelihood that you will be blessed by my potential.

True wisdom is understanding this interdependence: "The purposes of a man's heart are deep waters, but a man of understanding draws them out" (Proverbs 20:5). This cannot occur, however, if we are consumed by thoughts of ourselves.

SELFISHNESS DESTROYS PERSONAL HAPPINESS AND SATISFACTION

You were created to give. When you lavish your potential on yourself, your potential and all you accomplish by using it lose their meaning. King Solomon learned this when he went through life doing one thing after another for himself.

"Meaningless! Meaningless!" says the Teacher. "Utterly meaningless! Everything is meaningless." What does man gain from all his labor at which he toils under the sun?

I undertook great projects.... I made gardens and parks and planted all kinds of fruit trees in them. I made reservoirs.... I bought male and female slaves.... I also owned more herds and flocks than anyone in Jerusalem before me. I amassed silver and gold for myself....

I denied myself nothing my eyes desired; I refused my heart no pleasure. My heart took delight in all my work, and this was the reward for all my labor. Yet when I surveyed all that my hands had done and what I had toiled to achieve, everything was meaningless....

So I hated life, because the work that is done under the sun was grievous to me. All of it was meaningless, a chasing after the wind.

*I hated all the things I had toiled for under the sun, because **I must leave them** to one who comes after me.*

Now all has been heard; here is the conclusion of the matter: Fear God and keep His commandments, for this is the whole duty of man. For God will bring every deed into judgment, including every hidden thing, whether it is good or evil (Ecclesiastes 1:2-3; 2:4-8, 10-11,17-18; 12:13-14).

Work and effort that focus on self are meaningless. It doesn't matter what you accomplish, none of it will bring you satisfaction unless you give from what you have. Nor will your accumulated riches bring you happiness, for they are useless and meaningless if you don't understand and seek to fulfill God's purpose for giving them to you.

Work and effort that focus on self are meaningless.

You must share what you earn before it can bring you pleasure and satisfaction because sharing ensures that the blessings you have received will be passed on and others will also be blessed. This basic principle of sharing is foundational for maximizing your potential.

If you refuse to share, your potential will kill you because you cannot enjoy freedom in your conscience when you are acting against your natural design to give. *Pleasure will end, but conscience abides until it has completed its assignment.* It works on you until you acknowledge the error of your ways. Only by releasing all God has given you can you have a pure and holy conscience before Him and find meaning in life. Pursuing selfish pleasure always destroys the one who seeks it. In a similar manner, unshared potential consumes the person who seeks to hold it tightly for selfish gain.

SELFISHNESS DESTROYS THE JOY OF GIVING

First, selfishness destroys God's pleasure in watching you pass on all He has given you. Near the end of His life, Jesus reminded His disciples that they could not accomplish anything apart from Him. The same is true for our lives. Even as Jesus remained in fellowship and conversation with God throughout His life, so we must abide in Him. Without this consistent association with God, our fruitfulness suffers and we become no more than a branch to be thrown into the fire. The power of potential is gone. (See John 15.)

This absence of power hurts both the person who has withdrawn from God and God Himself. He created us to bear fruit that reflects His nature and glory. When we neglect to fulfill this purpose, we grieve the heart of God.

God's pleasure in Jesus was evident when He spoke from a cloud at the time of Jesus' baptism and again on the mountain of transfiguration (see Matthew 3:17 and 17:5). The source of His pleasure was Jesus' willingness to fulfill the purpose for which He had been sent into the world and to release His potential.

By Myself I can do nothing; I judge only as I hear, and My judgment is just, for I seek not to please Myself but Him who sent Me (John 5:30).

He who speaks on his own does so to gain honor for himself, but he who works for the honor of the one who sent him is a man of truth; there is nothing false about him (John 7:18).

The one who sent Me is with Me; He has not left Me alone, for I always do what pleases Him (John 8:29).

I have brought You glory on earth by completing the work You gave Me to do. And now, Father, glorify Me in Your presence with the glory I had with You before the world began. I have revealed You to those whom You gave Me out of the world. They were Yours; You gave them to Me and they have obeyed Your word.... All I have is Yours, and all You have is Mine. And glory has come to Me through them.... I am coming to You now, but I say these things while I am still in the world, so that they may have the full measure of My joy within them (John 17:4-6,10,13).

What was this full measure of joy that Jesus knew?

Let us fix our eyes on Jesus, the author and perfecter of our faith, who for the joy set before Him endured the cross, scorning its shame, and sat down at the right hand of the throne of God (Hebrews 12:2).

Obedience. Jesus found joy in doing what God asked of Him. The path of sorrows certainly did not bring Him happiness while He walked it, but He looked beyond the pain and shame to the reward of reclaiming His rightful place at the right hand of God.

This is also the source of God's pleasure in us. As we obediently share all that God has given us for the world, we will find that He delights in us. If, however, we decline to fulfill His plans and purposes and refuse to allow His nature and likeness to govern our thoughts and actions, we destroy the fullness of joy we could have brought Him had we sought His purposes and obeyed His principles.

Secondly, selfishness destroys the joy of giving. When we hoard and hide what we receive from God, we deny ourselves the delights of passing on God's gifts. The second letter of the apostle Paul to the church at Corinth reveals this delight.

> *Out of the most severe trial, their overflowing joy and their extreme poverty welled up in rich generosity. For I testify that they gave as much as they were able, and even beyond their ability. Entirely on their own, they urgently pleaded with us for the privilege of sharing in this service to the saints.... So we urged Titus, since he had earlier made a beginning, to bring also to completion this act of grace on your part. But just as you excel in everything— in faith, in speech, in knowledge, in complete earnestness and in your love for us—see that you also excel in this grace of giving* (2 Corinthians 8:2-4,6-7).

The Macedonian churches understood that sharing is a privilege to be sought and enjoyed. Therefore, they gave even when they had little. We do well to learn this same lesson. It is not the magnitude of our gift but simply the act of sharing that produces joy. When we refuse to share we deny ourselves this benefit.

Third, selfishness destroys the joy of seeing others share what we have given them. The apostle Paul also speaks of this joy.

> *In all my prayers for all of you, I always pray with joy because of your partnership in the gospel from the first day until now, being confident of this, that He who began a good work in you will carry it on to completion until the day of Christ Jesus* (Philippians 1:4-6).

Partnership speaks of sharing. When we fail to share our potential, this partnership is forfeited and the fruit for which we were chosen and appointed is lost.

You did not choose Me, but I chose you and appointed you to go and bear fruit—fruit that will last. Then the Father will give you whatever you ask in My name (John 15:16).

God mourns for this loss because the loss of potential limits His activity on earth and destroys the joy of sharing—for God, for ourselves, and for those with whom we might have shared. Selfishness always destroys the joy of giving.

SELFISHNESS DESTROYS THE GIFT

God is often hurt because people are pregnant with great treasure but they keep it to themselves. Say, for example, that you are a medical researcher who discovers a cure for leukemia. Instead of sharing the results of your research with others, you carefully guard your secret knowledge so no one else can take credit for your discovery. Meanwhile, many people needlessly die. In time, your God-given talent to heal will be destroyed. Because you are so concerned that someone may receive the recognition you deserve, you will lose the desire to study and to receive new medical insights. Your selfishness in keeping the treasure to yourself ultimately destroys the very gift that is the source of your wealth. *Potential that is not shared self-destructs.*

SELFISHNESS STOPS THE FLOW OF GOD'S BLESSINGS

Finally, selfishness destroys the cycle of giving initiated by God. Very often you have not because you lavish upon yourself all you have received. God will give you all things if you ask to receive so you may pass it on to others. I'm blessed because I have a passion to pass on to you all that God has given to me.

God expects you to pass on to another all He has poured into you. Get rid of it. Make room for more of the vast quantity He has prepared to pour into you. You hold up God's plans and purposes when you cling to your blessings, and you cap off your potential when you refuse to share all you have received. Jesus said:

Give, and it will be given to you. A good measure, pressed down, shaken together and running over, will be poured into your lap. For with the measure you use, it will be measured to you (Luke 6:38).

**God expects you to pass on to another
all He has poured into you.**

Some of you are blessed with tremendous talents, gifts, and knowledge. I wonder what is happening to them. Flow with your God-given abilities. Use them to bless others and to glorify God. Don't worry if your gifts and talents aren't as grand as you'd like. Use them to benefit others, and you will see them grow. *Sharing all God has given you is a must if you want to maximize your potential.*

∞ PRINCIPLES ∞

1. Potential cannot be maximized and fulfilled unless it is shared.

2. God shares with you so you can share with others.

3. Isolation is not good because it prevents sharing.

4. You must share your potential within the limits of God's laws.

5. Giving transforms and reveals potential.

6. God's blessings in your life expose His power within you and the possibilities that are your potential.

7. The selfish retention of God's gifts destroys:
- God's joy in giving,
- your personal happiness and fulfillment,
- your joy in giving to others,
- your joy in watching others share what they have received from you,
- the gifts that are given,
- the continuing evidence in your life of God's blessings.

8. Giving your potential to others is a basic key to maximizing all that God has given you for your blessing and the benefit of others.

CHAPTER SEVEN

YOUR POTENTIAL AND THE NEXT GENERATION

**To live for today is shortsighted;
to live for tomorrow is vision.**

Just as a seed has a forest within it, so we contain much more than is evident at birth. Everything is designed by God not only to reproduce itself but also to transfer its life and treasure to the next generation. Potential is not fully maximized until it reproduces itself in the following generation.

An old Chinese proverb that states, "the end of a thing is greater than its beginning," rings true for our lives. King Solomon concurred with this truth: "The race is not to the swift or the battle to the strong..." (Ecclesiastes 9:11b). Every individual is therefore responsible to live to the fullest for the sake of the following generation. King Solomon states it this way: "A good man leaves an inheritance for his children's children" (Proverbs 13:22a).

A Seedless Life

I will never forget the day I first discovered seedless fruit. One of the pleasures I enjoy within my very busy schedule is accompanying my wife to the food store, which gives us time to plan our family meals and discover new items together.

On one of these occasions, as we approached the produce section, I was intrigued to see a large sign introducing seedless grapes and oranges. At first I rejoiced at the prospect of being able to enjoy grapes for the first time without the inconvenience of having to eject the seeds. (No doubt this newly produced hybrid was developed in response to the market demand for fruit that could be enjoyed without the discomfort of seeds.) So I quickly picked up two pounds of red and white grapes and a bag of oranges, looking forward to eating them.

My impatience to experience the thrill of seedless grapes prompted me to place the bag of grapes beside me in the car so I could enjoy them while I was driving home. What a pleasure, to sink my teeth into fresh, juicy, sweet grapes without having to worry about seeds. It was like a dream come true. Soon after we had arrived home, I sliced into an orange and stood amazed at the fact of a seedless fruit. Again I experienced a new pleasure, sucking the juice from a seedless ripe orange.

Later that day I returned to the kitchen to enjoy the rest of my new discovery and to marvel at this feat of botanical science. Suddenly, in the midst of my pleasure, I was startled by this thought: "If these grapes and oranges have no seeds, how can they reproduce another generation of fruit?" After all, the life and power is in the seed, not the fruit. Immediately I realized that I was enjoying momentary pleasure at the expense of generational reproduction. The fruit was beautiful, ripe, sweet, juicy, and pleasing to eat, but it lacked the potential to transfer its uniqueness to another generation. *In reality the tree is not in the fruit but in the seed.*

Life and power is in the seed, not the fruit.

God created seeds to guarantee the fulfillment of future generations. Every plant, animal, bird, reptile, and insect possesses within itself the ability and potential to reproduce itself and to continue the propagation of its species. Consider then the prospect if every seed decided to germinate, develop into a beautiful tree, and have juicy, sweet, *seedless* fruit. What would be the result? A natural tragedy! Chaos would ensue and ultimately the genocide of mankind would follow as oxygen disappeared from the atmosphere for the lack of trees.

Please note that the seed in this example did fulfill part of its purpose. It germinated, grew, developed, and even bore fruit. Yet the totality of its potential was not fulfilled because it did not extend itself to the maximum potential of releasing seeds. Because the seed failed to reproduce itself, the next generation of trees was robbed of life, consequently affecting the entire human race and all creation. This is the impact when one element in nature withholds its true potential and refuses to maximize itself.

Tragically, there are millions of people who exist in "seedless lives." They are conceived, grow, develop; they dress up, smell good, and look good; and they even pretend to be happy. Yet everything they are dies with them because they fail to pass on everything God gave them. They have no sense of generational responsibility. They have no idea of their duty to the future. No man is born to live or die to himself. When a seed maximizes its potential, it not only feeds the next generation but also guarantees it through the seeds in the fruit.

No man is born to live or die to himself.

God gave you the wealth of your potential—your gifts, talents, abilities, energies, creativity, ideas, aspirations, and dreams—for the blessing of others. You bear the responsibility for activating, releasing, and maximizing this potential as a deposit for the next generation.

∾ THE SCHOOL THAT WAS ALMOST KILLED ∾

Several years ago I was invited to speak at a church conference in Gary, Indiana, on the topic of discovering your purpose in life. Before I was introduced, the host invited a gentleman to share briefly on the establishment of an educational institution that had distinguished itself in that community. An unassuming, middle-aged gentleman stepped forward and began to share a story that pierced my soul. He told of how his mother had failed in an attempt to abort him as an unborn child, and he had ended up living in foster homes all over the city for many years. He emphasized how he had dreamed of providing an environment in which young people could grow and learn so that they would not have to suffer what he had experienced. He introduced to the audience the school he had founded and established—a school that had become one of the leading academic institutions for high school students in that city.

Imagine if his mother had been successful. She would have killed a school. Despite his past and his less-than-ideal heritage, this dreamer rose above his circumstances and maximized his potential, which is now benefiting generations to come.

The prophet Elijah also exemplifies the importance of living to the fullest and refusing to settle for present circumstances. As recorded in the Book of First Kings, Elijah confronted the prophets of Baal and challenged them to a contest to prove that Jehovah is the true God. The test was to build an altar and call on God to send fire from the heavens to consume the sacrifice. After much prayer and dancing by the prophets of Baal, there was no response or results. Then Elijah began to call on the Lord God, and fire fell and consumed the sacrifice. Afterward, he commanded the people to seize the prophets of Baal, and all were destroyed. When Queen Jezebel, a worshiper of Baal, heard this news, she sent a message to Elijah, threatening his life.

Elijah was afraid and ran for his life. When he came to Beersheba in Judah, he left his servant there, while he himself went a day's journey into the desert. He came to a broom tree, sat down under it and prayed that he might die. "I have had enough, Lord," he said. "Take my life; I am no better than my ancestors" (1 Kings 19:3-4).

After all his great accomplishments and achievements, this distinguished prophet had a death wish with suicidal tendencies. God was not persuaded. He intervened and showed Elijah that he had much more to accomplish before his full potential and purpose would be maximized. Then God instructed Elijah to anoint the next kings over Aram and Israel, and more significantly, to anoint Elisha to succeed him as prophet.

Just suppose Elijah had died when he wanted to quit. His successor, Elisha, who performed twice as many miracles as Elijah, would not have discovered his purpose and fulfilled his potential. It is imperative, therefore, that we never settle for the average of our circumstances because there are thousands of "Elishas" waiting on our obedience to fulfill their lives.

∞ Maximizing Potential Is Dying Empty ∞

As I have stated in my previous books, the wealthiest place on this planet is not the gold mines, diamond mines, oil wells, or silver mines of the earth, but the cemetery. Why? Because buried in the graveyard are dreams and visions that were never fulfilled, books that were never written, paintings that were never painted, songs that were never sung, and ideas that died as ideas. What a tragedy, the wealth of the cemetery.

I wonder how many thousands, perhaps millions, of people will be poorer because they cannot benefit from the awesome wealth of the treasure of your potential: the books you have neglected to write, the songs you have failed to compose, or the inventions you continue to postpone. Perhaps there are millions who need the ministry or business you have yet to establish. You must maximize your life for the sake of the future. The next generation needs your potential.

The next generation needs your potential.

Think of the many inventions, books, songs, works of art, and other great accomplishments others in past generations have left for you and for me to enjoy. Just as their treasure has become our blessing, so our potential should become the blessing of the next generation. The apostle Paul in his letter to his young friend Timothy describes his life as a drink offering that was poured out for others.

For I am already being poured out like a drink offering, and the time has come for my departure. I have fought the good fight, I have finished the race, I have kept the faith (2 Timothy 4:6-7).

What a sense of destiny, purpose, and accomplishment is contained in these words. There is no hint of regret or remorse, only confidence and personal satisfaction.

Millions of the world's population, both now and in generations passed, have poured out some of their potential, accomplished some of their dreams, and achieved some of their goals. Still, because they have refused to maximize their lives, their cup holds a portion of their purpose, stagnating into depression, regret, and death.

I admonish you, decide today to act on the rest of your sleeping dream. Commit yourself to the goal of dying empty. Jesus Christ our Lord, at the end of His earthly assignment, gave evidence of His success in maximizing His life by fulfilling all God's will for Him on earth. As He journeyed to the place of crucifixion, many people followed Him, mourning and wailing. Seeing them, Jesus said:

Daughters of Jerusalem, do not weep for Me; weep for yourselves and for your children (Luke 23:28b).

The implication is evident: "I have completed My assignment, stayed through My course, and finished My task. I have emptied Myself of all My potential. Now it is your turn."

❧ Don't Be a Generational Thief ❧

First discover what you were born to be, then do it. Fulfill your own personal purpose for the glory of God. *Your obedience to God's will and purpose for your life is a personal decision, but not a private one*. God has designed the universe in such a way that the purposes of all mankind are interdependent; your purpose affects millions. Maximizing your potential is, therefore, necessary and critical. Your sphere of influence is much greater than your private world.

> **Your sphere of influence is much greater than your private world.**

Suppose Mary had aborted Jesus, or Andrew had failed to introduce Peter to Jesus. What if Abraham had not left the Land of Ur, or Joseph had refused to go to Egypt. Or let's assume that Ananias had not prayed for Saul who became Paul, or that the little boy had refused to give Jesus his lunch. How different the biblical record might read! These examples show that although our obedience is always a personal decision, it is never a private matter.

Don't rob the next generation of your contribution to the destiny of mankind. Maximize yourself for God's glory. Remember, he who plants a tree plans for prosperity. "The wise man saves for the future, but the foolish man spends whatever he gets" (see Proverbs 21:20).

⧉ PRINCIPLE ⧉

1. The life and power to reproduce is in the seed.

2. You rob your children when you withhold your potential.

3. You must maximize your life for the benefit of the next generation.

4. Potential is not fully maximized until it reproduces itself in the next generation.

5. Obeying God's will for your life and fulfilling His purpose is a personal decision, but not a private one because your sphere of influence is much greater than your private world.

CHAPTER EIGHT

UNDERSTAND AND OBEY THE LAWS OF LIMITATION

Freedom without law is anarchy. Liberty without responsibility is irresponsibility.

The morning sun shimmered brightly on the choppy waves of the bay as a small motor boat moved slowly over the water. Perhaps 200 yards away, 14 swimmers plied through the chilly waters. Twenty men and women had begun the race that morning, but six had been pulled from the water into one of the many boats that lined the course. Exhaustion, muscle cramps, or some other malady had taken them from the race even before the swimmers had reached the mid-way point.

Just now the swimmers were bunched more closely than they had been for some time. As the far shore came into sight the competitors appeared to reach into their resources and pull with greater power and precision. Between them and the beach lay their greatest test, an area of swift-moving currents that had carried many a swimmer far toward the sea before he had been rescued or finally had given up and drowned.

Of the 14 swimmers in the water, 13 had swum the bay before. They knew from experience the dangers of the currents. Although those who watched from the boats kept an eye on the veterans, it was the one rookie swimmer they watched most closely. Just now he was in the lead, several hundred yards ahead of the pack.

Would he heed the warnings and follow the instructions he had been given to swim up the coast a piece before attempting to cross the swift-moving channel? If he did, he would win the race easily. If he did not, thinking that he didn't want to waste the time to swim parallel to the shore, or that he was strong enough to meet the currents head on, they were ready to move quickly to rescue him. All watched anxiously to see what he would do.

As the rookie neared the buoys that marked the swift-running water, it appeared for a moment that he would stay within the marked course and swim upstream. He had not moved more than 20 yards, however, when he turned and swam directly toward the shore. Instantly, motors sprang to life and two boats sped across the water to the now-struggling swimmer. These were Coast Guard boats manned by experienced rescuers.

Later that afternoon when all the swimmers had reached the beach—including the rookie, who had been brought in by a Coast Guard cutter—the winner of the race approached the young man who had nearly drowned. "Why did you change your mind?" he asked. "The officials told me that you started to follow the path marked out for us, but then you suddenly veered toward the shore."

"Those 20 yards that I swam upstream against the current were so easy that I thought all the fuss about that channel was just so much hype. So I decided to cut through it to win the race by a large margin. I soon realized that not only wouldn't I win the race, I wouldn't even finish it. For an instant I felt so dumb for throwing away the race, but then I realized that I had jeopardized my life as well. I'll never try this again."

Oh, I think you should enter the race again next year," said the veteran racer. "You're a magnificent distance swimmer. Just follow the rules the next time and you'll find that the crossing point determined by the race organizers is challenging, but not life-threatening. Each year that point is different because the currents constantly change, so we all have to follow the prescribed course. One year we didn't race at all because the officials couldn't find a safe place to cross the channel. I wanted to talk them into sponsoring the race anyway, but I knew that would be foolish. Most likely no one would have finished anyway. Well, I hope to see you next year. It's about time someone beat me. For a while I thought this would be the year."

How sad! Although the rookie swimmer had the potential to beat the veteran, he lost the race, and nearly his life, because he chose to veer from the assigned course. He exercised his freedom to go his own way. This grasping for freedom is a universal tendency. To maximize your potential, you must understand the concept of freedom and the principle of law.

WE WANT TO BE FREE

The cry "We want to be free!" has swept our world in remarkable and frightening ways within the past decade. Particularly in Eastern

Europe, the desire for freedom has brought sweeping revolutions, toppling governments and power structures that have repressed and oppressed many peoples. This same yearning for freedom prompts pregnant women to abort their babies, children to take their parents to court, and students to seek greater control over the measures of discipline used in their schools.

Freedom! It sounds so good. Everybody wants freedom. Ethnic groups, social groups, religious groups. Children, youth, adults. All want the right to determine their own lives and to make their decisions without guidance or interference from anyone else.

It should not surprise us, then, that many common phrases express this craving for freedom: Freedom of the press, Freedom of choice, Freedom of religion, Freedom of speech. All reveal the universal longing to be unencumbered by the dictates and the decisions of others.

∞ Nothing Is Free ∞

Is this truly possible? Can we be entirely free? No, I don't think so. Nothing is free. Although advertising tries to convince us that we are getting something for nothing—buy one, get one free—we are still paying for the product the advertiser claims is free. In a similar manner, the cost of sweepstakes and prizes given to entice consumers to buy a particular product or to subscribe to a certain periodical is built into the company's price structure somewhere along the way. We cannot get something for nothing.

Nothing is free.
We cannot get something for nothing.

This axiom is also true in relationships. We cannot be entirely free to do what we want, when we want, where we want, how we want, and with whom we want. Freedom always has a price because the actions of one person restricts and influences the freedom of another. The woman who aborts her baby takes away the baby's freedom to live, and the student who slaps the teacher who reprimands her takes away the teacher's freedom to keep order in his classroom. Freedom without responsibility cannot be freedom for all who are involved.

⤜ The Consequences of Freedom Without Responsibility ⤛

Lawlessness is the freedom to do whatever we want, when we want, with whom we want, with no one telling us to stop. In essence, we defy the standards that govern society to become a law unto ourselves with no sense of responsibility toward anything or anyone.

For example, you may choose the freedom to smoke marijuana behind your house at three o'clock in the morning. You know you are breaking the law, but you choose to disregard the law and to exercise your freedom to do as you please. *Lawlessness always results in slavery, death, and the loss of preexisting freedoms.* Adam and Eve's experience in the garden verifies this truth. Freedom without law is bondage.

The Loss of Freedom

When God created the man and the woman and placed them in the garden, He gave them the following instructions:

You are free to eat from any tree in the garden; but you must not eat from the tree of the knowledge of good and evil, for when you eat of it you will surely die (Genesis 2:16b-17).

They were free to eat from any tree in the garden, but one.

When the serpent convinced the man and the woman to eat from this one tree, God put them out of the garden and they lost the freedom to eat from the garden's other trees. Their desire to be freed from God's restrictions cost them the freedom He had given them to eat from the other trees in the garden. Thus, *the first penalty of freedom without responsibility is the loss of existing freedoms.*

This proves to be true in all life. The teenager who stays out past his curfew loses his privilege to use the family car. The mechanic who charges exorbitant rates loses the customers he is in business to serve. The worker who takes 30 minutes for a 10-minute break loses the freedom to leave her desk without punching the time clock. The politician who forgets his campaign promises and breaks faith with the people who put him in office loses his reelection bid and the opportunity to serve his constituents.

SLAVERY

Slavery is a second consequence of freedom without responsibility. When the man and the woman disobeyed God and ate from the tree of the knowledge of good and evil, they became slaves to evil. Before their rebellion against God, Adam and Eve knew only good because their knowledge came from their relationship with God, who is good. In the moment of sin, their spirits became separated from God's Spirit and they became slaves of rebellion, the root of all sin. They could no longer see and do what God requires. This loss of the ability to see and do what is right is always a result of choosing to place oneself above the law.

Thus, the teenager who regularly stays out past his curfew comes to expect that this is his right, the mechanic who charges exorbitant rates loses sight of fairness, the worker who takes an extended break assumes the company owes her this, and the politician who breaks faith with those who elected him fails to see the error of his ways. Each becomes so enmeshed in his rebellious attitudes and actions that he can no longer see the wrong of his actions. Death inevitably follows.

DEATH

The third consequence of freedom without responsibility is death. Notice that God connected the violation of the boundary around the tree of the knowledge of good and evil with death: "...for when you eat of it you will surely die" (Genesis 2:16). Disobedience to law always results in death.

The teenager who indulges in late hours will eventually see the death of his parents' trust. The mechanic who takes whatever he can get will soon experience bankruptcy and the death of his business. Likewise, the worker who extends her break and the politician who neglects to fulfill his promises will suffer the death of their dreams for advancement and recognition. Death is the inevitable result of freedom grasped at the expense of obedience to law.

**Death is the inevitable result of freedom grasped
at the expense of obedience to law.**

∞∞ THE NATURE OF LAW, COMMANDS, AND DEMANDS ∞∞

Merriam Webster's dictionary (10th Collegiate, 1994) defines *law* as "a binding custom or practice of a community: a rule of conduct or action prescribed or formally recognized as binding or enforced by a controlling authority; a rule or order that is advisable or obligatory to observe." It further observes that *law* "implies imposition by a sovereign authority and the obligation of obedience on the part of all subject to that authority." Thus, a law regulates and governs the behavior of someone or something.

A *command* is an "order given" or an authoritative directive. It "stresses the official exercise of authority" and expresses the will of the authority based upon the established rules and regulations that govern the group. Thus, a *commandment* specifies behavior relative to a law.

A *demand* is "the act of asking with authority." It is based on the recognized authority of the one who asks, and it builds upon a previous command or commandment. Thus, a *demand* assumes that the requester has the right to make the request, and it specifies behavior in a specific instance or circumstance.

Let's use family life to illustrate these principles. As the head of the home, the father may establish the law that the privacy of each individual is ensured. This is a given within the structure of the family. Then he may issue the command that all members of the family should knock on a closed bedroom door and wait for the bidding "come in" before entering that room. This is his mandate or commandment relative to the principle of ensuring the privacy of each individual. Finally, when a daughter in the household is upset because her brother constantly enters her room when she is on the phone, the father may demand that the son knock on his sister's door and wait for her response.

∞ Law Provides Direction for Daily Life ∞

God has established many laws that influence our lives. Some of these govern the physical world in which we live; others control our relationships within the human family and with God Himself. For example, God has established marriage as the structure in which sexual relationships should be enjoyed and children should be raised. That is His law. "You shall not commit adultery" (Exodus 20:14) is one of His commandments built on that law. Hence, when God demands that you should not gratify your physical desires by engaging in intercourse outside the marriage relationship, He is applying to daily life the law He established at creation and the commandment He gave at Mount Sinai. He is specifying how we should behave in a given situation.

God's demands are always based on His laws and commandments. He is not capricious, nor is He out to destroy our pleasure. *He knows that we cannot fulfill our potential outside His laws*, so He gives us commandments relative to those laws and He makes demands on us that apply His commandments to our situation. If we resist His demands, we bring upon ourselves the natural consequences of His laws. The law of love is a good example of this principle.

God created us to be loved by Him and to love Him and others in return. Love is an innate quality of His nature and of ours. The commandments "Love each other as I have loved you" (John 15:12), and "Love your enemies and pray for those who persecute you" (Matthew 5:44b) direct our efforts to understand and apply that law of love to our lives. When we disregard this law, we bear the consequences of loneliness, alienation, and internal turmoil that naturally come to those who fail to love.

We cannot choose whether or not these consequences will come to us, since they are inseparable from the law. Our only choice is whether or not we will love. Thus, we see that God's commandment to love, like all His commandments, is given for our good. Those who obey it are spared the pain that irrevocably assails those who fail to love.

God's commandments are given for our good.

The effects of God's laws cannot be avoided. They are constant and unchangeable, even as He is. Yet, you control the impact of God's laws on your life because the decision to obey or disobey God's commandments and demands is wholly yours. In this manner, *you control your destiny.*

◯◈◯ READ THE FINE PRINT ◯◈◯

Nothing can function at its maximum performance if it violates God's laws or the laws laid down by the manufacturer. These laws set the boundaries or limitations within which all things must operate. There is no recourse. The preestablished consequences always follow the failure to fulfill the law's obligations.

If something sounds too good to be true, it probably is. Books and television shows may tell us that we are free to sleep around, but they don't caution us about the guilt and the misery that come from such actions. Pro-choice groups may persuade us that we are free to abort our babies, but they do not warn us of the severe depression and never-ending sense of loss that plague many women following an abortion. Cigarette ads may portray healthy, laughing men and women puffing away on the particular brand that tastes best and gives the most satisfying high, but they do not show the hospital rooms, cancer treatment centers, and doctors' offices filled with smokers suffering from lung cancer and emphysema.

Too often we resist obeying rules and living within a given set of laws, stipulations, and regulations because we see them as having a negative rather than a positive impact on our lives. The Scriptures are clear that God's laws are good. They are given for our benefit.

This is love for God: to obey His commands. And His commands are not burdensome... (1 John 5:3).

If you fully obey the Lord your God and carefully follow all His commands I give you today, the Lord your God will set you high above all the nations on earth. All these blessing will come upon you if you obey the Lord your God (Deuteronomy 28:1-2).

Your word is a lamp to my feet and a light for my path (Psalm 119:105).

Every commandment of negative orientation can be restated in a positive manner. "You shalt not misuse the name of the Lord your God" (Exodus 20:7a) could be rephrased, "Worship only Me." "You shall not steal" (Exodus 20:15) might be reworded, "Leave other people's possessions alone." "You shall not give false testimony against your neighbor" (Exodus 20:16) could be, "Tell the truth."

Unfortunately, mankind has difficulty obeying God's commandments. Therefore, God sets forth His commandments as prohibitions that set boundaries within which we must operate. He relates to us at the point of our sin and endeavors to move us beyond our failure and disobedience by giving us very specific guidelines and directions. Because Cain had already killed Abel, for example, God said, "You shall not murder" (Exodus 20:13) instead of "Honor and safeguard your neighbor's life." This same phenomenon is evident in the disciplining of a child.

Although the parent may tell the newly-mobile child "You may play only with your toys," she inevitably must add "Do not touch the stereo, the television, the magazines on the coffee table, etc." Do not touch...do not touch...do not touch. It is these negative statements that clearly define the child's boundaries and help him learn what is acceptable behavior and what is not.

So it is in your relationship with God. Through *thou shalt nots* God delineates the limits within which you can live a healthy, happy, productive life. They are His means of helping you. He does not intend to unnecessarily harm, restrict, or bind you.

God created you to fulfill your potential, but you must accept the principles and laws that govern it. That's the bottom line.

❧ MISCONCEPTION OF LAW ❧

The limitless ability God has given us to do all we can think, to accomplish all we can imagine, to fulfill every aspiration we entertain cannot survive unless we obey God's laws and live within His limitations. To encourage an accepting attitude toward God's laws and commandments, let us examine some of the misconceptions that surround the concept of law.

> **Our potential cannot survive
> unless we obey God's laws
> and live within His limitations.**

MISCONCEPTION—LAWS RESTRICT US

All parents have heard the complaint, "You just don't want me to have any fun," when they put a restriction upon their children's activities. Whether it is a curfew, a rule about calling home, or a standard that requires the child to avoid being at a friend's home if the friend's parents are not there, the child sees the rules and requirements as the parents' desire to withhold from him the enjoyable things of youth.

Very often we transfer this same attitude into our relationship with God. We see God's thou shalt nots as His means of taking the fun out of life. Then His laws appear to be restrictive instruments that limit our freedom to do what we want, when we want, where we want, with whom we want.

MISCONCEPTION—LAWS INHIBIT US

The misconception that law inhibits or restrains us also distorts our understanding of the purpose of law. This perception is readily evident in the attitude of the employee who feels that the obligation to punch a time clock cramps her preferred style of arriving at work five or ten minutes after the designated starting time and making up that time at the end of the day. Or perhaps a young couple believes that an apartment house's rule to rent only to married couples inhibits their freedom to live together. Or, yet again, a club that makes much of its income from a daily happy hour may consider an ordinance that holds establishments responsible for accidents involving their patrons unnecessarily prohibitive.

MISCONCEPTION—LAWS BIND US

Some laws appear to bind us and we, therefore, find them to be irritating. Traffic laws are good examples of these laws. One day as I rode in the car with my son, I tried to beat a yellow light because I was a little late. As the light changed, my son said, "Daddy, the light is changing." Just as I pressed the accelerator to make the light, he spoke again, "Daddy, you've got to stop," and then "Thou goest too fast, O Dad." Because I had taught him to stop at red lights, I slammed on the brakes and we came to a halt with a terrible screech. The law concerning red lights was particularly binding to me that day.

MISCONCEPTION—LAWS ROB US

The belief that laws prevent us from receiving the best things of life is also a false understanding of the nature of law. This perception often occurs when something we want defies a given law, but we want it anyway. A young Christian girl who wants to marry a nice-looking, well-behaved guy who isn't saved thinks God is unfair when He says not to be yoked with unbelievers (see 2 Cor. 6:14). A young businessman perceives himself to have been robbed when his partner is unwilling to use dishonestly obtained information to make a killing on the stock market. A single mother struggles between giving her tithe to God and spending the money on a much-deserved weekend away from the kids.

All these misconceptions convince us that laws and regulations are encumbrances and burdens that prevent us from enjoying life to the fullest. In truth, laws are provided for our benefit.

∽ THE BENEFITS OF LAW ∽

If, then, laws are given to help us and to make life more enjoyable, how do they accomplish their purpose? What reliable benefits do they offer?

BENEFIT—LAWS PROTECT

The child who lives with no rules and restrictions is much more likely to get hurt or to end up in trouble than the child who lives within a structure of parental guidance. Because he has no boundaries or guidelines against which he can judge his actions, he may make decisions that jeopardize his safety and well-being. The rule "no playing on the kitchen floor when Mom is making dinner," for example, protects a young child from being scalded. If he is not taught this rule, the child may not even know that he is in danger. Likewise, the restriction "no swimming alone" protects against drowning. In a similar manner, traffic signs such as stop, yield, slow, and detour have all been established not to restrict, but to protect us and others. Laws protect us. They alert us to possible danger.

Laws alert us to possible danger.

BENEFIT—LAWS ASSIST

Laws also give us assistance. Can you imagine the confusion if everyone addressed their letters however they wished? Some people might put the address of the sender in the upper left corner, but others might put the address of the recipient there. Or one community might have the tradition of putting the stamp on the back of the envelope, while every other community places it on the front. Postal regulations aid the efficient handling of mail so letters go to the sender's intended recipient. Instead of restraining us, laws provide assistance so we can accomplish what we intend.

BENEFIT—LAWS ALLOW FOR FULL EXPRESSION

Laws also allow us to express ourselves completely within the context of community. Consider what would happen if you bought a house in a nice neighborhood to raise your children in a safe, non-violent environment only to have your neighbor open an adults-only bookstore. The traffic on your formerly quiet street now quadruples and your children are exposed to unhealthy materials as people come from the shop leafing through pornographic literature. One night a patron is shot in front of your house by his wife, who is enraged by his attitudes and his actions toward her after he has been looking at his girlie magazines. Suddenly, your nice neighborhood is no longer safe. Civil laws help to control what is and is not permitted within a community so that all may enjoy the environment they desire.

Although these laws may irritate us because they compel us to act in a certain manner, they permit us to enjoy personal preferences within our personal space. Consider, for example, the following situation. A resident in an apartment complex enjoys listening to classical music, but the young man in the next apartment blares his rock music so loud that it rocks his neighbor's walls and drowns out her music.

If you are the young man who prefers loud rock music, the rules of the apartment complex that control noise appear to be restrictive and binding. For the person in the neighboring apartment, however, the regulations permit her to enjoy her own taste in music. *Laws allow each person to enjoy his individual preferences so long as he does not infringe on the freedom of others to do the same.*

BENEFIT—LAWS MAXIMIZE POTENTIAL

Laws help us to do and be our best. The very laws that restrict negative behavior also encourage and uphold positive attitudes and actions. The classroom rule, for example, that makes the entire class responsible for monitoring cheating and gives a failing grade to anyone who copies from another student's paper also encourages excellence because it exerts peer pressure for honesty and guarantees that each person will be graded by his or her own efforts. Thus, the law both sets consequences for negative behavior and rewards those who work hard and do their best.

> **The very laws that restrict negative behavior
> also encourage and uphold
> positive attitudes and actions.**

The Bible clearly shows that laws do not restrict positive thoughts and behavior:

...live by the Spirit, and you will not gratify the desires of the sinful nature. For the sinful nature desires what is contrary to the Spirit, and the Spirit what is contrary to the sinful nature. They are in conflict with each other, so that you do not do what you want. But if you are led by the Spirit, you are not under law.

The acts of the sinful nature are obvious: sexual immorality, impurity and debauchery; idolatry and witchcraft; hatred, discord, jealousy, fits of rage, selfish ambition, dissensions, factions and envy; drunkenness, orgies, and the like. I warn you...that those who live like this will not inherit the kingdom of God.

But the fruit of the Spirit is love, joy, peace, patience, kindness, goodness, faithfulness, gentleness and self-control. Against such things there is no law (Galatians 5:16-23).

Since the violation of law destroys potential, and ob_dience to law fulfills potential, law encourages the releasing and the maximizing of potential.

**Law encourages the releasing
and the maximizing of potential.**

BENEFIT–LAW SECURES PURPOSE AND FUNCTION

Finally, law allows us to function within God's general design for human life, and the plans and purposes He sets for our individual lives.

The blessing of the Lord brings wealth, and He adds no trouble to it (Proverbs 10:22).

Achieving purpose with God's blessing never brings sorrow. Those, however, who try to fulfill their potential outside His purposes often experience multiplied sorrow. A businessman, for example, who builds his business without God's guidance and direction may attain the same wealth as a man who submitted his dreams and plans to God's will, but his position outside God's plan does not provide the freedom from worry that the other businessman enjoys. Those who must rely only on themselves to protect their gain often become ill from worrying. There is no joy in that kind of wealth.

When the Lord blesses a person with prosperity, He both protects what He has given and He serves as a resource to the recipient. Man needs spiritual resources as surely as he needs physical and material assets.

∞ Your Potential Needs the Benefit of God's Law ∞

Potential without law is dangerous. Even as breaker switches cut off electricity when an electrical appliance malfunctions and a free flow of electricity is possible, so God shuts us down when we operate outside His laws. This is His safeguard to keep us from self-destructing.

Potential without law is dangerous.

Many people throughout history have harmed themselves and others because they tried to fulfill their potential outside God's specifications. Adolf Hitler, for example, was a gifted leader. Using his leadership skills, he came up through the ranks of government until he was legally elected the chancellor of Germany. Once he achieved that position, something went wrong. He violated the rules of leadership.

Power is always given to work through the vehicle of servanthood. When we are in a position of authority, we have the responsibility to serve those under us. Hitler violated that law and made himself a dictator. Instead of using his power to serve and bless the country he ruled, he placed himself above the law and forced people to do his bidding.

Hitler also broke the laws of human dignity and equality because he created and enforced policies that treated all people who were not of Aryan descent, with blond hair and blue eyes, as subhumans and half-humans who were created to serve the perfect race. Many Jews and other non-Aryan peoples were victims of Hitler's beliefs and policies. Eventually he brought death to himself and those who shared his convictions.

Potential is always given to bless, never to harm. If your potential is hurting someone or something, you'd better look carefully at your attitudes and actions. You are probably using your gifts and talents outside their God-given specifications.

∽ Potential Dies When Laws Are Broken ∽

The experience of Hitler and many other people confirms that the violation of the boundaries that delimit potential sets off serious consequences and exposes the violator to potential-threatening circumstances. This is true because violating the specifications set forth by God for the use of potential removes protection, hinders fulfillment, and interrupts performance.

Let's say, for example, that you are a young executive in a local bank. You have worked for the bank for five years, developing a good working knowledge of the banking industry and building a solid reputation for honesty and integrity. Your goal is to become the manager of the main branch.

Your spouse constantly complains that you don't earn enough until one day, in desperation, you take $2,000 from the bank safe and give it to your spouse. Several things happen when you do this. First, you lose the protection of your good reputation. Until now, people have trusted not only your integrity but also the soundness of your decisions. Second, you forfeit the opportunity to rise to the position of branch manager. Third, you interrupt your career because not only the bank you worked for but other employers as well cannot trust you. This one act of disregarding the commandment "You shall not steal" (Exodus 20:15) destroys your potential to become a competent, respected banker.

Jesus came to recover the spirit of God's laws so we can recognize them as the blessings they are, and to show us the power that belongs to those who live within their God-given specifications. Only by the power of the Holy Spirit can we live within God's laws of limitation and, thereby, maximize our potential. Laws and limitations established by a manufacturer for a product are always given to protect and maximize the product's potential and performance, not to restrict it.

Flipping a switch is a helpful way to use electricity. Sticking your finger in a socket is not. Even as you cannot live if you ignore the precautions that govern the safe use of electricity, so you cannot experience the full, abundant life Jesus promises if you disregard the specifications that limit the use of your potential. You must abide by God's specifications to enjoy the totality of who you are. His laws and commandments are the security that guarantees you will receive all He planned and purposed for your life.

A man without God is potential without purpose.
A man without God is power without conduction.
A man without God is life without living.
A man without God is ability without responsibility.

That's a dangerous man.
That's a live wire.

∽ PRINCIPLES ∽

1. Freedom always has a price. What frees one person may enslave another.

2. Lawlessness defies the standards that govern society. It shows no responsibility toward anyone or anything.

3. Lawlessness results in the loss of existing freedoms, in slavery, and in death.

4. Laws set norms or standards and govern or regulate behavior.

5. Commandments express the will of an authority relative to a law.

6. Demands specify behavior in a specific situation based on previously defined laws and commandments.

7. Violating laws and commandments aborts potential and brings inevitable consequences.

8. Laws and commandments benefit us and have a positive impact on our lives.

CHAPTER NINE

RECOVERING YOUR POTENTIAL

**It is always better to fail at something than to
excel at nothing. Get up and try again.**

A hush fell over the room as a petite, neatly groomed woman stepped to the podium. Unlike most of the others in the room, she was not clad in prison-issued attire. Yet she did not seem to be or to feel out of place. Those who watched her wondered at this, for they had observed many people in these weekly meetings. Most had a genuine desire to help the prisoners, but their actions and remarks often revealed that they were uneasy being there and that they did not truly understand what imprisonment did to a person. Although the prisoners were grateful for the concern and well-meaning of these visitors, they preferred those speakers who were comfortable within the prison walls. They often understood more accurately the particular needs and frustrations that prison life produced.

Expectancy filled those who faced the woman on the stage. Although they could not define why, they sensed that this speaker was different from the rest. She didn't look any different, yet she *was*

189

different. Perhaps it was the gentle compassion in her face as she looked out over the women who packed the small room. Perhaps it was her calm, assured manner that revealed an absence of fear or nervousness. Perhaps it was that she did not place any notes on the lectern. For whatever reason, the prisoners knew that this speaker was unlike the others who had come to encourage and strengthen them.

Her first words startled them. "I am one of you. I lived here for five years. I came here at the age of twenty, leaving behind my husband and my young daughter. Although it has been many years since my release, I still remember the intense loneliness and the consuming despair that filled my first days here. I can also hear in my mind the click of the gate behind me. I doubt those thoughts and feelings will ever leave me.

"I am here today because something very important happened to me here. I met the Lord Jesus Christ, accepted His forgiveness for my past, and entrusted my future to His keeping. My life is very different because of Him. Through His love and mercy, and the support and encouragement of many brothers and sisters in Christ, I have finally forgiven myself for the wrongs that brought me here. Today I am free because He freed me, and I bring to you the opportunity to find this freedom and forgiveness.

"When I first came here, I hated myself. All my life, my family told me that I would never amount to anything. I believed them. When I landed in jail, I fulfilled their prophecies and my own expectations. I assumed that the rest of my life would continue to follow a similar pattern. I learned, however, that they were wrong, and I was wrong. Through the patience and faithfulness of those who helped me to survive within these walls and to make it on the outside, through my study of the Bible, and through my personal relationship with Jesus Christ, I have discovered that I am capable of far more than my family expected of me.

"This is true because God created me for a special purpose and placed within me the potential to fulfill all that He planned for my life before I was born. The unfavorable circumstances that surrounded my birth did not change God's intentions, nor have the wrong choices, broken relationships, and painful experiences of my past destroyed who I yet can be. The talented, worthwhile person with distinct abilities that I have learned to see in myself was inside me all the time, but I had to discover her and release her from the guilt and self-hatred that consumed me throughout the early years of my life.

"I have also learned that my experience is not unique. The world is filled with men and women whose experiences parallel my own. Both in my counseling practice and after speaking engagements, I have spent hours listening to and sharing with people whose hearts and lives are as burdened as mine were when I first entered these walls. Jesus Christ has given me compassion for them and for you. He has also gifted me with the ability to express that love and concern in a wide variety of settings.

"Therefore, I come to you today as a friend who wants to help you become all that you can be. *No matter what others have said about you, and what you have believed about yourself, you are a competent, gifted person.* I know you may not feel that way, but your feelings are not accurate. You are the beloved daughter of God, created by Him with meticulous care and endowed by Him with everything you need to bless yourself, your family, and, indeed, the entire world. This potential hibernates within you, buried by the actions, attitudes, and lifestyles that brought you here, but it need not remain hidden. *You can recover your potential.*

"I share my story with you not because I have made it by society's standards, but because I have a passion to free women like us—women who have been bound not only by prison walls but also by years of negative opinions, poor judgments, unhealthy relationships, detrimental environments, and adverse circumstances. I stand with you as one who has found the way to peace, happiness, and fulfillment. Perhaps my story can help you find that way as well.

"I was born..."

Few stirred throughout the lengthy story. Occasionally someone nodded her head in agreement or sighed from memories awakened by the storyteller's words. At times tear-brightened eyes overflowed from pain remembered or hope renewed. These were largely unnoticed, for all were caught up by the story of one whose life in some ways paralleled their own and in other respects was quite different. Hopelessness, bitterness, resentment, anger, and despair were certainly part of her story, but they were not the dominant themes. Woven within the story of what the ex-prisoner had been were glimpses of what she had become and yet hoped to be. There were no dramatic adventures or shocking disclosures, just the simple retelling of the changes in a life touched by the love and power of God.

Many women in that small room yearned for the trust and the contentment evident in the speaker's words as they wondered whether their lives could also be redirected into the plans and purposes of the

Creator. Was there hope for their potential yet to be revealed? As the speaker closed with a simple testimony to her current life in Jesus Christ, many hearts longed for the assurance that they too could experience changed, redeemed lives.

Change. The hope for something different. Each of us, at some point in our lives, has been dissatisfied with where we are and who we are. We have been keenly aware that life is not measuring up to our expectations. Some of you may still be there. Others of you, like the former prisoner, have found renewed hope in life. *A life-changing encounter with God through His Son Jesus Christ makes the difference.* The Bible teaches us much about our need for this life-changing encounter and the path we must take if we would experience it.

∞ FORGIVENESS ∞

The journey to recovering your potential begins with forgiveness— God's forgiveness and self-forgiveness. God's forgiveness is an expression of His love for us. He offers it to all who confess their rebelliousness and accept His gift of new life through His Son, Jesus Christ. Becoming rerooted in God takes care of this first aspect of forgiveness.

Self-forgiveness, however, is often more difficult. God forgives and forgets our sin as soon as we confess it:

The Lord is compassionate and gracious, slow to anger and abounding in love. He will not always accuse, nor will He harbor His anger forever; He does not treat us as our sins deserve or repay us according to our iniquities. For as high as the heavens are above the earth, so great is His love for those who fear Him; as far as the east is from the west, so far has He removed our transgressions from us (Psalm 103:8-12).

We, on the other hand, often hold ourselves accountable for our wrongs for a long time. Indeed, many who have accepted Jesus Christ as their Savior still think and act as though their sins are not forgiven. Such behavior short-changes potential because it again places ourselves above God and His word to us. Like Adam and Eve in the garden, we disbelieve what God has said.

The speaker in the prison must have been guilty of some rather serious wrongs to land herself in prison, but her journey to happiness and wholeness began with her ability to accept God's forgiveness and to forgive herself. In a similar manner, the apostle Paul could have condemned himself forever for the Christians who died by his hand (see Acts 7:54–8:3; 9:1-2). Praise God, he did not!

Remember, God's promises are true and His power surpasses all other powers. *If God says your sins are forgiven, they are forgiven. You are freed forever from their penalty and their power over you. No one, including satan, has the authority or the right to change or dispute His decision.*

The failure to forgive ourselves places us at risk for future sin. This is true because self-condemnation opens the door for satan and his forces of evil to work on us with doubt and guilt. Guilt prevents us from actively seeking God's power and wisdom because we are ashamed to enter His presence, and doubt enslaves us to feelings of powerlessness and unworthiness. Both deny the power and authority of God in our lives and entice us to rely more on our feelings than the presence of God's Spirit within us. Both destroy potential.

Refuse, then, to allow self-condemnation to steal your potential in Christ. If you have confessed your sin, you are forgiven and God remembers it no more. Forgive yourself and move on. If you would love others and share your potential with them, you must first love and forgive yourself. This is an important step in the journey of recovering your potential.

⚮ YOUR PAST AND YOUR POTENTIAL ⚮

A second step in recovering potential is the ability to move beyond your past and to use it to inform and improve your future. All of us have things in our pasts of which we are ashamed. While self-forgiveness takes away the sting of those confessed sins, it does not remove from our minds the memory of those wrongs. We must learn to live with our memories and allow them to be a positive force in our lives.

**We must learn to live with our memories
and allow them to be a positive force in our lives.**

King David, after his sin with Bathsheba, most certainly was haunted by his wrong (see 2 Samuel 11:1–12:25). Overwhelmed by the enormity of his sin, he could have forfeited his potential to serve God as the king of God's people. Instead, David confessed his sin (see 2 Samuel 12:13 and Psalm 51) and petitioned God:

Create in me a pure heart, O God, and renew a steadfast spirit within me.... Restore to me the joy of Your salvation and grant me a willing spirit, to sustain me (Psalm 51:10,12).

Today David is remembered as a man after God's heart and the greatest king in the history of God's people.

This same restorative power of God can move you beyond the negative opinions, poor judgments, unhealthy relationships, detrimental environments, and adverse circumstances of your past. No sin is too great for God to forgive. No relationship is beyond His restoration. His healing touch can reach into your worst experiences and show you something you can learn from them. His transforming power can redirect your misguided and harmful actions and enable you to remove yourself from the destructive environments and crippling circumstances that threaten your potential. No memory is too deep for Him to heal. No problem is beyond His blessing and power.

No sin is too great for God to forgive.
No relationship is beyond His restoration.
No memory is too deep for Him to heal.
No problem is beyond His blessing and power.

The key to moving beyond all that haunts you from your past is allowing those memories to empower you instead of destroying you. If you were addicted to drugs and you know firsthand the destructive forces they unleash, use your experiences to help those who are at risk today of experiencing the same pain you've survived. Make friends with a teenager whose father has walked out on his family. Support a local teen's club. Speak in your child's school about the dangers and the deceptions of doing drugs.

If you have a history of getting into fights, learn what sets you off and how you can respond more appropriately to the anger-provoking situations in your life. Find supportive people who can encourage you and help you through tough times. Look for the insecurity in yourself and others that destroys self-esteem and incites verbal and physical exchanges.

If you quit high school because you were pregnant, go back to school and get your diploma. If you did time in prison, befriend a newly released prisoner. If the pressures of being a young single mother caused you to abuse your child, offer to help another young mother who is going through experiences similar to your own.

Discouraging, defeating experiences may be part of your past life, but there is no reason why they must continue to discourage and defeat you. Indeed, they can become stepping stones to the releasing and max-imizing of your potential if you are willing to acknowledge your past, to learn from your mistakes, and to allow God's transforming power to turn your loss into gain. With God's help, you are capable of rising above your shortcomings and of redeeming your less-than-perfect decisions. He has not given up on you. He's waiting to see what you will do with the rest of your life. Protect the present and the future from the past by facing the past and moving beyond it. This is an essential element of the journey to recover your potential.

❧ REDEEMING THE DAYS OF YOUR LIFE ❧

The third step to recovering our potential is to redeem the time that is left to us. We cannot undo what is past, but we can make the neces-sary changes in our lives to permit the wise use of the remainder of our days.

Time is God's gift for accomplishing our purpose and fulfilling our potential. It begins the day we are born and ends when we die. The length of our physical life matches the days required to fulfill our purpose because God planned for the maturing of our lives within the total days He has allotted to us. Therefore, we have sufficient time to maximize our potential. The question is, Will we waste or use wisely the days God has assigned to our lives?

**Time is God's gift
for accomplishing our purpose
and fulfilling our potential.**

The apostle Paul instructs us to "see then that [we] walk circumspectly, not as fools but as wise, redeeming the time, because the days are evil" (Ephesians 5:15-16 NKJV). In other words, we must find our purpose and use our potential to accomplish it. Likewise, we need to consciously refuse to allow procrastination, discouragement, and the other enemies of our potential to induce us to waste even one day of our lives. Whenever we use our time to do things that neither release our potential nor help us progress toward the accomplishment of our purpose, we forfeit or delay the opportunity to reach the excellency and completion God intended for our lives.

Accepting God's forgiveness and forgiving yourself, moving beyond your past, using your past to inform the future, and redeeming the remaining days of your life are the necessary factors that will permit you to recover your potential. Like the former prisoner who forgave herself for her past and used it to bring life and hope to others, you can replace the hopelessness, bitterness, resentment, anger, and despair in your life with peace, happiness, and fulfillment. Her journey of recovery began when she met the Lord Jesus Christ and accepted His forgiveness for her past. You too must begin to recover your potential by accepting Jesus as your Savior and by allowing Him to change you. Return to your Manufacturer/Creator for a reassessment of your true potential and begin again.

You can replace the hopelessness, bitterness, resentment, anger, and despair of your life with peace, happiness, and fulfillment.

Just as a seed is full of promise and potential, so your life is abundantly loaded with untapped power and purpose. Likewise, just as a seed needs to be related to the soil and to be fed nutrients to maximize its fullest potential, so you are in need of a personal relationship with the Source and Creator of your life. Only God the Father can restore you to your original purpose and dream, and only He can provide the grace and resources you need to experience true fulfillment. Every product needs to remain related to the manufacturer if it is to maintain its guarantee and warranty. Therefore, I encourage you to obey the call of God in your heart right now by pausing before you read any further and praying this prayer of submission and commitment:

Dear Heavenly Father,

I confess that You are the Creator and Sustainer of my life. I believe that You created me for a specific purpose, and that You have designed and equipped me with the potential to fulfill that purpose. I admit that I have attempted to live my life without Your Spirit and guidance; I ask for Your forgiveness for this rebellious spirit. I acknowledge the work of reconciliation You accomplished through the death and resurrection of Christ Jesus for my personal restoration, and I receive Your Spirit to live within me now. By faith in Your promise, I receive with thanksgiving a new beginning as I commit myself to pursue the fulfillment of Your will for my life and the maximization of the potential You have invested in me.

In the name of my Lord, Jesus the Christ,
Amen.

If you prayed this prayer, you have joined millions around the world who are part of the great Body of Christ. Write to me and let me know of your decision today. (See the address for Bahamas Faith Ministry on the copyright page.)

**It is more important to be yourself
than to be the best.**

∞ PRINCIPLES ∞

1. God created you for a special purpose and gave you the potential to fulfill it.

2. You are a competent, gifted person.

3. You must experience a life-changing encounter with Jesus Christ if you want to recover your potential.

4. The journey to recovering your potential must include:
- accepting God's forgiveness,
- forgiving yourself,
- moving beyond your past,
- using your past to inform your future,
- redeeming the remaining days of your life.

CHAPTER TEN

POTENTIAL AND GOD'S PURPOSE

**Until a man can see beyond his own loins,
the future is in danger.**

God created everything for a purpose and equipped each created thing with the corresponding potential or ability to fulfill that purpose. All of nature testifies to this great truth, as is evidenced by the fact that seeds always carry within themselves the germ of the trees they were destined to produce. In every bird there is a flock, in every cow a herd, in every fish a school, and in every wolf a pack. Everything is pregnant with the potential to become all it was created to be.

The release and maximization of that potential is dependent, however, on an environment that is conducive to its development and release. For instance, despite the potential of a seed to produce a tree after its kind, and to bring forth fruit in abundance, this great potential can be minimized, restrained, or immobilized by an improper environmental condition. If the seed is placed on a baked clay tile or a stone, or in a polluted substance or toxic elements, its great potential will be restricted and never fully maximized.

This limitation of potential not only robs the seed of the right to fulfill its true potential but it also robs birds of food and of branches for their nests, and deprives people of wood for building houses, of fruit for food, and of fuel for heat and cooking. In essence, this loss of potential due to an improper environment interferes with the entire ecological system. The seed fails to produce a tree, which is prevented from producing oxygen to give life to men, who are then incapable of fulfilling God's will and purpose in the earth. Therefore, any attempt to restrict, abuse, misuse, oppress, or repress the potential of any living thing has a direct effect on the purpose and will of God.

∞ A WORD TO THE THIRD WORLD ∞

The magnitude and depth of human potential on earth has yet to be tapped. Millions are born, live, and die, never discovering or exposing the awesome potential that resides within them. This tragic state of affairs, which is a global phenomenon, is the result of man's succumbing to life governed by his own devices. The major source of this tragedy is ignorance.

The most powerful enemy of mankind is not sin or satan, but this death-dealing, life-stealing force called ignorance. The Old Testament prophet Hosea recognized ignorance as the primary source of personal, social, and national destruction. When relaying God's explanation for moral and social decay among the nations, he wrote, "My people are destroyed from lack of knowledge" (Hosea 4:6a). The implication is that destruction in any area of our lives, whether personally or nationally, is related to a lack of knowledge.

**The most powerful enemy of mankind
is not sin or satan, but ignorance.**

This reality is profoundly true as it relates to the maximization of our potential. The ignorance of mankind concerning the value, worth, and magnitude of human potential causes massive oppression of our wonderful treasure.

Our planet is now home to over 5.8 billion people, all of whom are "created in the image of God" and possess the potential to fulfill the purpose for which they have been born. Over 4 billion of these people live in countries and conditions described as *Third World*. The term *Third World* is not ethnic or racial in orientation, but is more philosophical and conditional in meaning. Technically, it is used to describe any people who have not been allowed to participate in or directly benefit from the industrial revolution, and who therefore have not directly profited from the social, economic, and technological advancement that accompanied this revolution.

In practical terms, the term *Third World* categorizes all people who, for whatever reason, have been robbed of the opportunity to discover, develop, refine, release, and maximize their God-given potential. This miscarriage of justice has often been the result of oppression and suppression, and it is usually generated by discrimination, prejudice, hate, and fear. Many of these forces of oppression are institutional, constitutional, philosophical, and religious in origin, but all are founded on grave ignorance and misconception.

The ignorance of man about man is the ultimate cause of all our problems. The key to the knowledge of any product must be the manufacturer because no one knows a product like the one who created it. Therefore, the truth about man cannot be found in the great libraries of our educational institutions or the journals of our scientific investigations.

Genesis, the first book of Moses, clearly states that God created man to dominate the earth:

Then God said, "Let Us make man in Our image, in Our likeness, and let them rule [have dominion] over the fish of the sea and the birds of the air, over the livestock, over all the earth, and over all the creatures that move along the ground" (Genesis 1:26).

The ignorance of man about man is the ultimate cause of all our problems.

Please note: God created all men to dominate the earth, not one another. *Therefore, every human possesses the ability and the potential to dominate, rule, govern, and manage the earth.* Each one has within him the spirit of leadership and the aspiration to determine his own destiny. This sacred spirit must be respected, protected, and properly related to God, the Creator, or its power will be turned toward other men to oppress them.

This has been the plight of all Third World people. They have fallen victim to the ignorance of men concerning the equality and purpose for mankind. We have all been created to serve the purposes of God as partners in dominion over creation, for the purpose of manifesting God's nature and Kingdom on earth as it is in Heaven.

Jesus the Christ came into the world for this reason: to restore us back to our Creator/Father God through His atoning work so that we can rediscover our rightful place within His will for His creation—not to create a religion. This great message, called the gospel, has been contaminated by many for their personal motives and has even been used to justify oppression and suppression in many cases. Therefore, it is imperative that we in this generation commit ourselves, our resources, and our energies to destroying the ignorance and error that cloud the truth concerning mankind, God's crown of creation.

You are so valuable and necessary to the destiny of the human race that God chose to come to earth Himself to redeem you to your purpose and true potential. What you were born to do and be caused Jesus Christ to come to give His life for your reconciliation. The world needs your potential.

The world needs your potential.

Nothing is more tragic than the waste, denial, abuse, and suppression of human potential. The millions of Third World people in Europe, Asia, Africa, and the Americas, including those who are quietly buried within the walls of the industrial states, must now determine to loose themselves from the mental shackles of the oppressor; to honor the dignity, value, and worth of their brothers; and to provide an environment within which the corporate will and energy of the people may be developed. We must chart a new course based on the principles of the Kingdom of God that will harness the intellectual resources, spiritual virtues, and economic industry of our people and will provide a national incubator that will encourage the maximization of the potential of generations to come.

The choice is yours.
You are responsible to understand, release,
and maximize your potential.

∞ PRINCIPLES ∞

1. Everything God created is equipped with the potential or ability to fulfill its God-given purpose.

2. You cannot maximize your potential unless you live in an environment that is conducive to its development and release.

3. Potential can be minimized, restrained, or immobilized by an improper environment.

4. Your potential is lost when you try to live by your own devices.

5. Ignorance steals life and deals death.

6. You possess the ability to dominate and manage the earth.

7. You are valuable and necessary to the destiny of the human race.

Books by
Dr. Myles Munroe

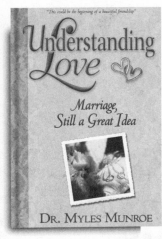

UNDERSTANDING LOVE: MARRIAGE, STILL A GREAT IDEA

In this frank, honest, and insightful book, Dr. Myles Munroe cuts through the fog of ignorance and misinformation to illuminate marriage as God designed it; a pure and holy institution in which a man and a woman enter into a commitment to become "one flesh," as equal partners in a lifelong union of friendship and companionship.
ISBN: 0-7684-2154-3

COMING IN THE WINTER OF 2002

UNDERSTANDING LOVE BOOKS 2 & 3

UNDERSTANDING YOUR POTENTIAL
ISBN 1-56043-046-X

RELEASING YOUR POTENTIAL
ISBN 1-56043-072-9

MAXIMIZING YOUR POTENTIAL
ISBN 1-56043-105-9

SINGLE, MARRIED, SEPARATED & LIFE AFTER DIVORCE
ISBN 1-56043-094-X

IN PURSUIT OF PURPOSE
ISBN 1-56043-103-2

THE PURPOSE AND POWER OF PRAISE & WORSHIP
ISBN 0-7684-2047-4

THE PURPOSE AND POWER OF GOD'S GLORY
ISBN 0-7684-2119-5

Available at your local Christian bookstore.

Additional copies of this book and other book titles from DESTINY IMAGE are available at your local bookstore.

For a complete list of our titles, visit us at www.destinyimage.com Send a request for a catalog to:

Destiny Image® Publishers, Inc.

P.O. Box 310

Shippensburg, PA 17257-0310

"Speaking to the Purposes of God for This Generation and for the Generations to Come"